THE MULTIPLE
POWER I OFFENSE

Rhod Reaves

PARKER PUBLISHING COMPANY, INC.

West Nyack, N.Y.

Library of Congress Cataloging in Publication Data

Reaves, Rhod,
   The multiple power I offense.

   Includes index.
     1. Football--Offense. I. Title.
GV951.8.R44   796.33'22   75-30579
  ISBN 0-13-604942-7

Dedication

To My Late Father, Vic Reaves
who coached football for 38 years

and to My Late Grandmother, Maggie Reaves
who raised us both and lived to see
us combine 55 years of coaching

FOREWORD

Here are a few brief but important facts regarding our high opinion of Coach Reaves based upon our observations and actual working contacts with him.

Coach Reaves has consistently shown much responsibility to the football program, the school, and the community. He is well known and well liked by a large majority of people in the Ritenour District. Coach Reaves has "lived" for Ritenour and its athletic programs. We recall that he willingly took over as temporary basketball coach while the regular coach was on service leave. Rhod has been willing to experiment with the squad in recent years for the express purpose of making it possible for a maximum number of boys to participate, while at the same time improving the overall performance of the squads. He has built a fine program. The teams have been very competitive and consistent winners. Ritenour teams have often won the "big ones" from top clubs in the area. In checking our data, we find that Ritenour has played more boys per game on the average than any other school in the conference.

Coach Reaves knows the game of football well. He has had a number of articles published in national athletic magazines. His teams are well coached and well disciplined. Desire, enthusiasm, pride, and spirit mark his players. They execute well and are intense. His players have always been gentlemen on the field and have shown maturity in victory or defeat. There has never been any poor sportsmanship at Ritenour.

Athletics in general and football in particular may be the last bastion of real self-discipline and direction. Psychologists tell us that young people today actually want discipline from someone . . . or somewhere. Athletics provide a place of belonging, where sacrifice and self-attainment can be realized. Coach Reaves has provided these positive benefits for the young men at Ritenour who have chosen to play football. He is a fine coach and a gentleman.

We have all been exposed to, and have a deep respect for, his "Multiple Power I" that he presents in this book.

Suburban North Coaches
St. Louis, Missouri

Bob Johnson, McCluer High School
3 League and 2 State Championships

7

Jerry Nordmann, Riverview Gardens High School
   4 League Championships

Bob Stouffer, Hazelwood High School
   1 League and 1 State Championship

Jim Veech, Normandy High School
   1 League Championship

Jerry Dwyer, McCluer North High School

The Advantages of the Multiple Power "I" Offense

This offense blends a combination of the speed and deception of the current wishbone attack, and the power of the single-wing. These two combinations require the integration of only three basic running techniques. These three techniques can be run out of 48 formations without creating a new learning situation for the offense. Through multiple deployment this offense takes advantage of the defense in one of two ways. It can either overload the defense or shift it out of position, attacking the weaknesses that are left.

This book also includes a two minute offense that has repeatedly scored two and three touchdowns in the fourth quarter to come from behind and win. This complementary attack is known as the "Quick Draw Offense." It can be easily installed with any system. The Quick Draw Offense has proven to be the most exciting tactical adventure that we have experienced.

This book is for coaches at all levels. It is aimed at any coach who uses the triple option play sequences and wishes to take it well beyond the present times with mutliple deployment. It is aimed at any coach who wishes to expand his "I" system. Even a pro-coach should be able to read the Quick Draw Offense with considerable interest.

All coaches should be aware that their personnel should blend in with their tactical system. At a college or pro-level, a coach can pick his personnel to fit his tactics. At the high school or lower level, a coach must adjust his tactics to fit his personnel. All successful offenses blend these two ingredients. There have been failures because coaches became so involved in their tactical plans that they did not realize their personnel was not tailored to their X's and O's. Any coach who lasts a decade will find himself in this situation and be forced to change. Don Faurot at the University of Missouri provides a classic example of this. He went from Paul Christman, his All-American single-wing tailback, to the invention of the split "T" in a very short time. This was because he was forced to adjust his tactics to fit his personnel. The Multiple Power "I" System is programmed to do just this.

This system is very simple for the players putting it into application, while it appears complicated to the outside observer. This is because of the unique method of splitting series to get multiple sets and their shifts from the fullhouse power "I" backfield. The backfield has only three basic techniques to learn. They are coordinated behind three types of blocking rules. These rules have been integrated through synonymous terms and techniques, and are run out of both balanced and unbalanced lines.

A fullhouse power "I" backfield set is the same as that of a wishbone set and you can run the triple option backfield sequence out of it to both sides without any difference in timing. You can also run "I" formation isolation plays which are an outgrowth of an almost completely disappearing single-wing.

Today's football is very specialized and sophisticated. We have many variations of the "I" formation with emphasis on power and passing. We have the wishbone with emphasis on speed and running. Both approaches are popular and are keeping the defenses busy. This book offers a simple system for integrating both approaches. The 70's should be a very interesting decade for both the offense and the defense. This is because we are seeing it all, and offenses seem to be taking on more individuality in their styles and systems.

Our Multiple Power "I" System is innovative and different. Not only have we integrated techniques and expanded them through multiple application, but we can adjust our tactics to fit our personnel and the times. Our multiple sets are determined by series. The personnel we have on hand determines the series of plays we run. Since our shifts and series of plays are tailored to fit our personnel we can change them from week to week or year to year. Times, personnel, and tendencies will determine that change. We keep it flexible and only change in the framework of the system. This is a step by step explanation of that system.

Rhod Reaves

The Author's Acknowledgement

As I begin to collect and focus my thoughts for the material to be presented, I realize we are basically talking about a combination of eighty years of coaching experience involving two other men.

Thirty-eight of those years belong to my Father, Vic Reaves. He was from the old school and used the unbalanced singlewing. His total record was 198 wins, 89 losses, and 27 ties. In 1953 he was selected the "National Prep-Coach of the Year." The Portageville, Missouri Football Stadium was dedicated in his honor, and named the Vic Reaves Athletic Field.

From the age of six I was raised by my grandparents in the small cotton town of Portageville, Missouri. Here football was a way of life and only second in importance to the cotton industry. As I approached high school age my Grandmother wrote my Father telling him, "Rhod and his friends are getting out of hand." Soon after that he accepted the football job at Portageville. You might say I knew him as my coach, before I knew him as a Father. For this I can now be grateful. What really charted my course was he gave me the responsibility of calling plays while participating as a pulling guard out of his singlewing. This was a time when most of the opposition was switching to the split-"T." As a result I became an enthusiastic student of the game.

I appreciate coach "Frosty" England for giving me the opportunity at Arkansas State University and introducing me to his rolling "T." Later as a defensive end at Southwest Missouri State University, I was thankful for the confidence that coach Fred Thomsen had in me and the encouragement of coach Aldo Sebben.

After two years in the Army I returned to Portageville as an offensive line coach. I wanted to install rule blocking for my Father's unbalanced lines. Fixing the positions of the set and applying the rules was my first innovative experience. Vic Reaves gave me much more than a singlewing background. He taught me a sound coaching philosophy and a lot of psychology. Most of all we finally developed a very close father-son relationship while coaching together.

After this I felt I was ready to become my own coach. I had no way of knowing then that I was about to meet a second man who was going to have an equal influence on my coaching career. I will be forever indebted to the opportunity that he gave me.

John Moore was the head wrestling and football coach at Ritenour High School. He won 14 straight State championships in wrestling. From the University of Missouri under the coaching of Don Faurot he become one of the pioneers of the split "T" in the St. Louis area. He was a master organizer of large programs. It was at a time when the Oklahoma types of defenses were catching up with the split "T." John was looking for a change. I became his offensive line coach. My second innovative experience was to help him convert tactically to a winged "T." It seems so little compared to what he taught me. I cannot begin to tell you how "country" I was or how much I had to learn about a big organization. As a result I become very program minded.

After John became a full time athletic director, I became the head coach. The blocking rules had already been integrated. In order to integrate backfield techniques we changed to a full-house power "I" backfield set. To get mutliple sets we changed from numbering our backs to a split-series call. We were the first power "I" team in the St. Louis area. In its first year we had an 8-1 record which is te best in Ritenour history.

Our most widely accepted innovation is the Quick Draw Offense. It is a two-minute catch-up offense that has repeatedly proven itself. Chapter 13 is devoted to it.

Last of all, I am deeply indebted to our coaching staff who have contributed to make our platoon program work. They are: Kin Lavender, Bill Green, Mike McIntyre, Gary Powell, Keith Leigh, Jim Moore, and our two Junior High coaches and staff, Paul Giebler and John Verby. We were all soon rewarded with two consecutive Suburban North Co-Championships.

If this book can help some coach with his tactics, adjust from a small to a large school, or keep abreast with the times—then I will feel the writing of this book was more than worthwhile.

CONTENTS

THE MULTIPLE
POWER I OFFENSE

CHAPTER 1

Developing the Multiple
Power "I" System

In developing a multiple offense you must first identify the elements that you have to work with. You can put multiple elements in two general classifications: techniques and formations. Different techniques put emphasis on different tactical characteristics. Those different tactical characteristics are speed, power and finess. When you can combine these three characteristics you have multiplied the element of techniques. The other multiple aspect is to achieve many formations or sets for your personnel. To develop a multiple system you must use logic in organizing your multiple thoughts.

MULTIPLE THINKING

Any time you can have two contrasting experiences, there will be both good and bad points for each. If you can recognize the good and the bad, you can eliminate the bad and maintain the good. It takes an innovative person to relate and integrate all the good points that were maintained from any two contrasting experiences. Football tactics can be approached in the same way. You can put things in categories of twos so you can simplify and compare. You can then put tactics into their proper perspective. Many coaches will eliminate the good points as well as the bad if they are not accustomed to the system. By comparing you should be able to relate what you are doing and what other coaches are doing, regardless of the differences in your methods and systems. You do not have to change your system to integrate the good ideas of another system into your way of doing things. You simply need to compare and relate. From here on when I use the term "we," it will include you as far as you are interested in comparing and relating to your own situation. This system is probably very different from what you are accustomed to, but I am sure you will be surprised to find many ideas that will relate to your problems. This system is a result of single lessons being learned from contrasting tactical experiences.

We will use a definite format for the presentation of material that follows. First, we will compare things by identifying the advantages and disadvantages, eliminating the disadvantages, and then integrating the advantages. Second, all step-by-step procedures will be put in categories or sequences. Third, when illustrations are used they will be designated as figures. When there is a sequence within a single figure, these will be called diagrams. This is necessary because of the step-by-step multiple aspect of our power "I" system. It will make it easier for you to understand.

TWO CONTRASTING INNOVATIONS AND ONE LESSON LEARNED

Assistant coaches can assume the role of innovators or they can be their own worst enemies. Some head coaches have their way of doing things, and if successful, are not interested in doing it another way. Any good head coach, however, will be interested in improving his own system. If you have a better way, he will be willing to listen. Any assistant coach can find something wrong. If he really knows football he will find a way to improve the present system. If he feels it should be done an entirely different way, then he himself has a lot to learn. Improving another man's system should offer a challenge to any good assistant coach. Many of the best innovations are those of assistant coaches.

As a player, I was first exposed to the unbalanced Warner's singlewing. Later, in college, I was introduced to the split "T." While participating, I had mixed emotions about these two contrasting systems. I had experienced the good and the bad of both. As a player I related most of my success to the singlewing. At that time I never related tactics to the limitations of my abilities. With the singlewing I was very successful as an offensive player, but with the split "T" I was only successful as a defensive end stopping the option. Once while playing defensive end, I had a bad experience against a singlewing. They just kept coming, and by the third quarter they were beginning to get to me. If I had not later seen the movies I would swear to this day they were using a 22-man offense. After that experience I vowed to become a singlewing coach forever. It was a narrow view from a player's eye level which was to later change when I became a coach.

My first coaching assignment was as an offensive line coach for an unbalanced singlewing. My first innovation was to install rule blocking for the unbalanced lines. My next coaching assignment was as an offensive line coach for the split "T." My second innovation was to integrate the blocking rules which contributed to our successful transformation to a wing "T" team. We will now examine these two contrasting innovations so we can compare and then relate to their influence in the development of the multiple power I system.

I do not know what your point of view is, but it is important for you yourself to know. I can put your thinking in one of three categories. You think one way or another or somewhere in between. Regardless of the way you think you should find something different that can apply to you in these two following contrasting problems and innovative solutions that we experienced over a decade ago.

The first problem (Figure 1-1) I faced was as an offensive line coach for the unbalanced singlewing both left and right. There was always a double team block and seal to the inside of the point-of-attack. The strongside guard would pull to the hole and kick out or lead. The weakside guard and strongside tackle could pull back to trap or seal. I wanted to install simple rule blocking. The unbalanced lines caused breakdowns and problems even if we flip-flopped them. I felt that

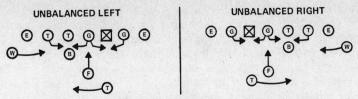

FIGURE 1-1: FIRST PROBLEM SINGLEWING

when you flip-flop the whole line you have a strongside tendency and are not as effective back to the weakside. I also felt that after you flip-flop, the strongside is not as effective to the left as to the right. I have seen some exceptions to this way of thinking. The need was to find a way to fix the sets in the line so we could have but one set of blocking rules that would cover both sides.

The first solution (Figure 1-2a) was to set the center of the line on the strongside guard. We changed his name to a middle guard. We set our even holes to his right and our odd holes to his left. We set the tackle and center to either side of the middle guard. These are the only two positions we would flip-flop depending on whether we were unbalanced left or right. We fixed the sets of the left and right guard. This fixed the sets of all our pulling offensive linemen. The middle guard could pull to the call and kick-out or lead at the point-of-attack. The left or right guard from the call could pull and trap or seal. To go unbalanced left we flip-flopped our center right and our tackle left (Figure 1-2b). To go unbalanced right we flip-flopped our center left and our tackle right (Figure 1-2c, This fixed the sets of our line so that we could apply simple rule blocking. This led to two conference championships using the singlewing attack.

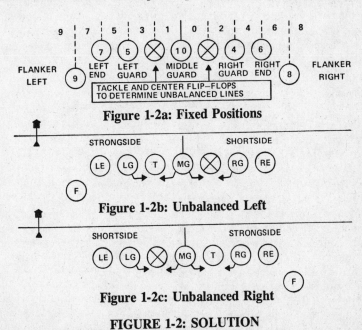

Figure 1-2a: Fixed Positions

Figure 1-2b: Unbalanced Left

Figure 1-2c: Unbalanced Right

FIGURE 1-2: SOLUTION

The second problem occurred when I became an offensive line coach for a split "T" offense. We used an inside gap-on-near linebacker, priority rule. The Oklahoma 54 defense was forcing us to add trap rules. We were pulling our guards. Their linebackers were keying our guards. There were some breakdowns in our rules. Our guards were not as well schooled in our trap techniques as their linebackers were with their keys. There was poor timing between the speed of our backs and the slow development of holes in our line. There was confusion between the two sets of rules. We needed to integrate them.

The second solution (Figure 1-3) was to switch the positions of our guards and tackles. Now our tackles pulled. We used a gap, double-team, seal at the point of attack. Any linemen between the call and pulling tackle used his inside gap, on, near-linebacker rule. The results were amazing. We were no longer confused and the defenses were. Our offense exploded. In a short time we had successfully changed to a winged "T" team.

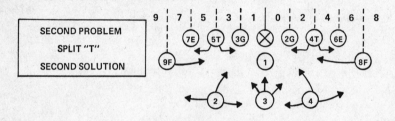

FIGURE 1-3

THE LESSON LEARNED from this is that you can mix oil and water if you mix them the right way. If you can integrate singlewing and split "T" techniques you can have a balance of speed and power. From these two contrasting experiences we learned to integrate our blocking rules with the aid of related terminology. Basically these are the same blocking rules that we use today with our power "I" offense.

THE REASONS FOR CALLING IN SERIES

Doing a few things well is a good theory as long as an offense does not spread itself so thin that a good technique defense is able to set. If players are able to run only a few plays from many sets without creating a new learning situation for the offense, then the defense cannot set. The same play can be run from many formations, forcing the defense to make numerous adjustments while the offense is still doing the same thing.

Many systems call the formation before or after the play. By calling in series we can integrate both the calls of the plays and formation. We like to be able to run all of our plays from a basic full house "I" backfield set. With the use of the shift we can then deploy our ends and wingback into multiple sets. Any offense that calls in series and uses simple blocking rules should be able to install a multiple offense.

The other method for calling plays is the numbering of the backs. This is a good method unless you want to use multiple formations. It can become very complicated since you have to have a different call for each formation. With four backs you will have to use four digits to designate each back; with a series call you need only one digit which can designate a dual meaning.

Now let us examine the advantages and disadvantages of the two methods used in a numbering system so we can compare them. By doing this we can see why we recommend the use of a series system over the numbering of backs to get multiple sets.

Regardless of what your numbering system is for calling plays there are basically only two approaches. In the backfield you can either number your backs, or call in series. In the line you can either number your offensive linemen or your defensive players. Let us compare these so we can see the advantages and disadvantages of each.

I. *Numbering backs* is usually related to the numbering of defensive players after offensive linemen have been numbered to designate a point-of-attack.

   a. *Application*—the first digit tells which back is to carry the ball, and the second digit tells the hole he is to carry the ball through.

   b. *Advantages:*
     1. Simple for coaches to understand.
     2. Prevents having too much offense.
     3. It is the most popular and widely accepted.

   c. *Disadvantages:*
     1. Limits types of blocking rules in the line.
     2. Limits number of techniques and plays.
     3. Makes the calling of multiple sets complicated.
     4. Backs often are forced to read the holes.

II. *Series* is usually related to the numbering of offensive lineman.

   a. *Application*—The first digit tells the backfield technique or pattern. The second digit tells both the hole and who is it get the ball.

   b. *Advantages:*
     1. Simple to coordinate backfield and line.
     2. Concentrates on the technique instead of the play.
     3. Can integrate techniques.
     4. Can run one play out of many formations.
     5. Can adjust your offense to fit your personnel.
     6. Can adjust your tactics to defensive tendencies.

   c. *Disadvantages:*
     1. The majority of coaches who are more familiar with the numbering of backs are slow to accept series calls.
     2. Danger of having too much offense.
     3. Calling many formations without a purpose.

For the players one method is as simple to learn as the other. It only depends on what they become accustomed to. Since we are a multiple offense, we use the series system as our method to call plays.

THE BIRTH OF THE MULTIPLE POWER "I" OFFENSE

To complete the ingredients for our offensive system we have to select a basic backfield set that we can coordinate behind both split "T" and singlewing types of blocking rules. We have four reasons for using a fullhouse power "I" set as our basic backfield formation:

1. We can simply change the offensive tendencies from one side to another by flip-flopping our wingback to a left or right halfback set. The sets of the quarterback, fullback and tailback remain fixed.

2. The set of the tailback is ideal for timing behind our singlewing type of blocking.

3. The set and timing of all four backs are almost identical to the wishbone set to our backside. It is a natural position from which to run the triple option sequence.

4. It is the best set we know of to shift to other formations for fast deployment.

We have now established all the elements that we will need for a multiple power "I" offense. We have integrated blocking rules. We have a backfield set that is a natural position for coordination wtih those integrated blocking rules. We have a series method of call and the shift to get multiple formations. Now we need to install the system for putting these elements into application.

SECONDARY ZONES

We have divided the field into five zones from the line of scrimmage to our goal line. Moving clockwise they are: Able, Baker, Charlie, Dog and Easy (Figure 4). Able is the left deep third of the field; Baker is the middle deep third of the field, and Charlie is the right deep third of the field. Dog is the short right side of the field and Easy is the short left side of the field. We use these five zones as points of reference in carrying out both our running and blocking assignments. We mention them now only because they are used with our numbering system. The zones take on more importance when we get into our passing system. The numbering of our holes as a point-of-attack will now be emphasized. Let us study our numbering system for calling plays.

HOW TO CALL THE PLAYS

Our method of calling plays is in four parts. We use two digits followed by two words. This is basically a two-phase call with only one thought pattern for each individual player. The first digit represents the series and formation set; the second digit represents the ball carrier and point-of-attack. The first word represents the type of play, indicating both the backfield pattern and blocking rule. The second word indicates the set of the split end. This call is simply "split left" or "split right."

Now let us take a look as to how we use this method of calling the plays:

1. *The series* are indicated by the first of the two digits. We call 10 through 90 series. It tells the backfield the techniques and patterns they are to use in the running of a play. It also tells the formation set from which to run the play.

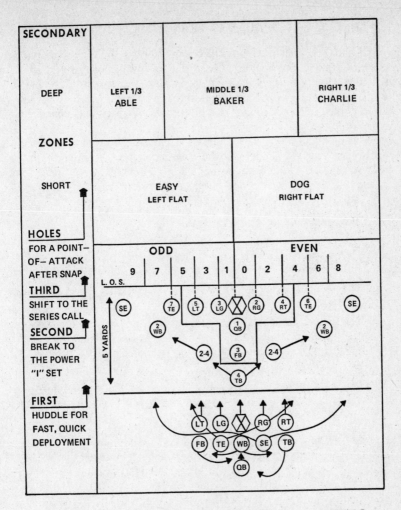

FIGURE 1-4: THE MULTIPLE POWER "I" SYSTEM

2. *The holes* are indicated by the second of two digits (Figure 1-4). To the left are 1 through 9 odd holes; 0 through 8 even holes are to the right. The holes tell both the backs and linemen the point-of-attack. It also tells the back whether he is to get the ball or not. All backs' patterns will cover certain holes. If a back's hole is called, he gets the ball. If another hole is called, he still runs his pattern without the ball. This is very often a fake depending on the technique.

3. *The types of plays* are indicated by the first word. We use three basic types of running plays. These calls are *powers, tandems* and *sweeps*. They have a double meaning. They tell the backs the techniques they are to use and the linemen the blocking rules they are to apply. This helps to coordinate the backfield with the line and assures that the correct backfield techniques will be used with the proper blocking rules.

USING THE HUDDLE

Our huddle is of the utmost importance for fast multiple deployment of personnel. From the side line our huddle (Figure 4) appears to be very much like many huddles used by others. Its big difference is the positions of the backs and ends and the routes they take to their sets after the break. This permits fast deployment of our flip-flopping ends and gets our wingback to the correct side of a full-house "I" backfield set.

Let us examine the total function of our huddle from the positions in the huddle to their sets. Any huddle is where the pre-plan of attack takes place. We have 25 seconds to do this and put the ball in play without being penalized. At this center of strategy we need a fast means of deployment. This makes the positions in the huddle very important (Figure 4):

1. The center lines up seven yards from the ball wtih his back to the line of scrimmage.
2. The guards and tackles line up in their respective positions so that the full interior line can turn on the break and go directly to their sets.
3. The wingback lines up in front of the center facing the quarterback. On the break he steps forward and swings to the side to which he is called.
4. The tight end and split end line up to each side of the wingback. On the break they turn and go directly to their sets as called.
5. The quarterback waits for the wingback to clear and follows the center directly to the line of scrimmage.
6. The fullback and tailback are positioned on the flanks. On the break they step towards the quarterback and then turn and follow him to the line of scrimmage.

This results in a very rapid break from the huddle to the power "I" sets (Figure 4). Basically we set in full house "I" backfield and go directly on the snap. We can also shift out of the power "I" to other backfield formations.

THE SHIFT

The team always breaks from the huddle directly to a power "I" backfield set. The series call determines if there is a shift to another backfield formation. This involves four men (Figure 4). Most of the time it is the wingback and tailback; occasionally it is the tight end or full back. The tailback can shift to either halfback set as called. Sometimes he is called to a flanker set. The wingback can shift from his halfback set to the flanker set on the same side. There are occasions when the tight end shifts to a split set, and the fullback shifts to a halfback set. Anytime the fullback shifts, the tailback will shift into his place. The series always predetermines the set.

THE SNAP SIGNAL

We use a non-rhythm count in our snap signal since the rhythm count may cause individuals to jump off sides. At a clinic I once heard Duffy Daugherty say, "Any obstetrician can tell you that the rhythm method does not always work." Our snap signal is in two phases; for example: "30 set"—"Hate

1''—"Hate 2." There is a delay between each phase to break the rhythm. The snap is a result of sound.

1. The first phase is before the shift or set, and has a dual meaning. The call can be 20,21,30 or 31 set. The first of the two digits indicates if the defensive secondary is two deep or three deep. The second digit indicates if it is an even or odd defense. This is determined by the offensive center being uncovered, or having a down defensive guard on him. After the word "set" the quarterback is responsible for the delay, so the team can get a proper shift and set.

2. The second phase is the sound for the snap. It can be either on the first or second "Hate." Again there is a delay between "Hates" to break rhythm and leave time to register a thought pattern. This cuts down on mistakes.

A PREVIEW OF MULTIPLE APPLICATION

As stated earlier we only have three types of running plays. They are: *powers, tandems* and *sweeps*. Basically we only have three things to learn to do. It is possible for us to take these three things and run them out of 48 formations without creating a new learning situation for ourself. We probably could never use this much offense within a year's time. We have game plans. Personnel, situations, times and defensive tendencies determine what we will use or not use.

THE PREVIEW:

Let us pull one play out of the hat so that you can examine the possibilites of what is to come (Figure 1-5):

1. In the huddle the quarterback calls a play, "96 sweep, split right." After a repeat and delay he then gives the snap signal "on second hate." After a repeat he claps his hands and says "break" (Figure 5). This shows the immediate deployment of the team to a power "I" backfield set to the weakside of an unbalanced line.

2. At the line of scrimmage the quarterback checks the defense. It is three deep with a middle guard over center. He yells the first phase of the snap signal "31 set." This already alerts the coach that it is a possible 52 monster, and that the only adjustment made to our unbalanced line is with the monster. This is where we use our communications system with the press box.

3. The word "set" tells the backfield to shift to their series call. The wingback shifts left to flanker set from his halfback set. The fullback shifts to a right halfback set. The tailback shifts to the fullback set. It is the quarterback's responsibility to see that the correct set is achieved before the snap of the ball.

4. After the snap both the backs and line apply the 6 sweep-slant techniques. The quarterback fakes the sweep to the tailback. He leaves the ball extended for the wingback to take it on a slant into the 6 hole. What makes this play effective is that the blocks cannot be keyed. The only difference from an 8 sweep is the lead guard traps. When the ball is snapped, it appears to be 8 sweep blocking.

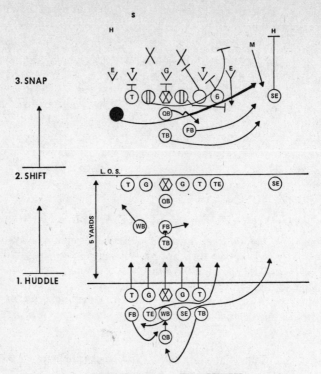

FIGURE 1-5: PREVIEW

In conclusion, this is confusing to persons on the outside. They may know what you are doing, but they don't know how and when you are doing it. Once you understand and become accustomed to it, it is very simple. This is a preview of the *Multiple Power "I" Offense*, and of what is to follow.

We will use a step-by-step procedure in the chapters that follow to make it easy for you to understand how we put our system into application. First we will show how we apply our blocking rules. We use three sets of blocking rules and integrate them through related terminology and techniques. Second, we will show the three basic backfield techniques we use in our running patterns; then coordinate the backfield techniques and blocking rules through synonymous terms. Next we will explain how we split our series to get multiple formation; finally, we will put it all together with the multiple application of all three types of running plays.

This system may seem complicated but it is simple when you put it into application and become accustomed to it. We have never seen our players have any problems learning our system. Occasionally a few coaches have had problems understanding it because our system is so different—it is like teaching an old dog a new trick. With players it is easy to teach a new dog a new trick: they become accustomed to it, and don't know any other system.

CHAPTER 2

How to Integrate the
Blocking Rules for
the Multiple Power "I"

The most important phase of any offense is the blocking rules. This is the part of the offensive system that can not afford to break down. You can change from one backfield pattern to another without effect on the system, but to change your blocking rules is to change your system. Adapt your backfield patterns to fit your blocking system. If you start trying to change your blocking schemes to fit a change in your backfield, your system will be in big trouble. Here you will need a simple system of blocking that will cover about any situation. Be careful not to start making too many exceptions to blocking rules: if you are making too many exceptions, then your rules are breaking down.

Our blocking rules have remained basically the same over the past 12 years. Outside of a few minor adjustments, this is the only part of our system that has not changed with the times. Our blocking rules have taken care of all our needs and changing situations without breakdowns. We have integrated two contrasting sets of blocking rules which are outgrowths of the singlewing and split "T." This has been done through related techniques and terminology. The terminology that is covered in this chapter is of the utmost importance. We use a third set of rules which is a combination of the other two. This gives us three blocking schemes that can handle just about any backfield pattern or sequence we might wish to install. Our offensive linemen have had no problems learning them and it has left their thinking free to prefect their techniques. Our opponents point to our blocking in the line as our biggest asset. We have a reputation for always having an offensive line.

We have three sets of blocking rules. They are *power, tandem,* and *sweep* rules. The *power* rules consist of straight ahead blocks for the fullback handoff and option plays. The *tandem* rules have double team blocks with isolations at the point-of-attack. The *sweep* rules are a combination of traps and sweeps to get wide. We integrate all three rules through techniques and terminology. This simplifies our learning situation and gives us every variation of blocking that we need.

FIXING THE HOLES ON THE OFFENSIVE CALL MAN

The odd holes are to the left of the center, and the even holes are to his right (Figure 2-1). When calling the play the second digit in the call will be the number of the hole. We can flip-flop our tight end and split end to get multiple line sets.

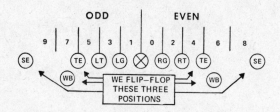

FIGURE 2-1: NUMBERING OF THE HOLES

We fix the holes by numbering the offensive linemen (Figure 2-2). The center's number can be either 1 or 0, the tight end's number can be either 7 or 6, and the wingback's number can be either 9 or 8. The left tackle is the 5 call man; the left guard the 3 call man; the right guard the 2 call man, and the right tackle is the 4 call man. This fixes the hole on the offensive linemen's outside hip regardless of where the defense is set.

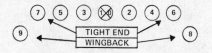

FIGURE 2-2: CALL MEN

In using splits in our line, we try to avoid anything that is not necessary (Figure 2-3). We maintain a two-foot split between guards and center and between ends and tackles. The variation in our splits are between tackle and guard. The tackle will take as wide a split as he feels he can while handling a defensive player in his inside gap at the same time. The better and faster he is, the wider his split. He must make this adjustment on the set.

FIGURE 2-3: SPLITS

TRIAD BLOCKING TERMINOLOGY AND TECHNIQUES

Blocking terminology (Figure 2-4) is the key to integrating our three types of blocking rules. If we can understand our terminology and relate it to our techniques and the call man, there should never be confusion that causes a breakdown. Let us define our basic terms (Figure 2-4):

1. *Reach* is to block the defensive man on the line of scrimmage who is set on your inside adjacent offensive lineman (Figure 2-4).

2. *Inside gap* is the defensive lineman on the line of scrimmage who is set between you and your adjacent lineman. From the center to the backside of the line he is termed as in an "outside gap." *The gap always has priority in all blocking rules* (Figure 2-4).

3. *On* is the defensive down lineman with whom you would make contact by moving forward (Figure 2-4).

4. *N.L.B.* is the nearest linebacker to you looking from the inside out in relation to the call (Figure 2-4).

5. *Cut-off* is to lead step toward the call filling the hole left by a pulling lineman (Figure 2-4).

6. *Puller* lead steps to the call to trap or seal at the point-of-attack (Figure 2-4).

7. *Post block* is done by the inside adjacent lineman to the call man. He posts the defensive man on or off the line of scrimmage in an area for the lead man. *Remember! his gap has priority over his post block* (Figure 2-4).

8. *Lead* block is done by the call man when his number is called as a point-of-attack. He blocks the first man to his inside who is set on or off the line-of-scrimmage (Figure 2-4).

9. *Seal* block is done by the first man to the outside of the call man. He blocks the first man off the line-of-scrimmage to the inside of the hole. The seal man could have already been set in that position or could have pulled to get there (Figure 2-4).

10. *Call man* has some relationships that need to be made with the three types of blocking rules:

    A. *On tandem* or sweep rules any offensive lineman to the outside of the offensive call man blocks the near inside man off the line-of-scrimmage.

    B. In our power rules the backside ends and tackles check and release. This is to screen the defense man in your immediate outside area and go down field and block the secondary to the call side. As a point of reference we use the names of the zones (Figure 1-4). If the backside ends or tackles are set left, they go to Dog to pick up the defensive backs out of Charlie and Baker. If the backside ends and tackles are set right, they go to Easy picking up the defensive back out of Able or Baker.

C. The terms backside and frontside pertain to the side of the wing-back. The terms shortside and strongside pertain to the set of the tight end, or unbalanced lines. Do not confuse these terms.

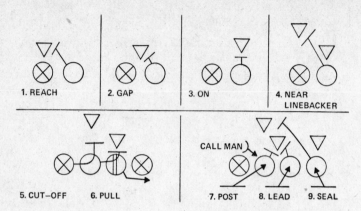

FIGURE 2-4: BLOCKING TERMINOLOGY

Once you understand our terminology and master the techniques you will have no trouble in putting all three blocking rules into application. Power, tandem and sweep blocking rules are very different in their function, but they are very much alike through their terminology and techniques.

POWER RULES

Power rules are related to speed. I realize this conflict in terminology which might be confusing, but this is the way they were originally termed with the split "T" offense and have never been changed. With power rules we only need three of our basic terms and one technique (Figure 2-5). Each frontside man must use the following order of blocking priorities: *gap, on* and *near linebacker*. The backside men check and release. We only need four holes we call to run our power plays. We make 2 and 6 calls to the right, and 3 and 7 calls to the left. *Even calls* (2 and 6 Powers) *are to the right* (Figure 2-5). Here are the rules as they are applied by each position:

1. *Split End*
    a. *Set right*—The mirror block is to run toward the defensive halfback as if he is running a pass pattern. He gets as close to him as possible without self-commitment. He tries to do everything the halfback does forcing him to commit himself. This is prefected with the use of a mirror drill in practice.
    b. *Set left* he checks and releases. He goes directly to Dog-zone to pick up the first man to come out of Baker-zone.
2. *Tight end* only blocks a man on the line of scrimmage if there is an inside gap situation.
    a. *Set right*—On a 2 call he blocks the near linebacker looking inside

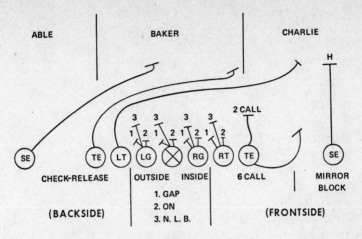

FIGURE 2-5: EVEN POWER RULES, 2-6 CALLS

out. On a 6 call he pulls right picking up the first man off the line of scrimmage in pursuit.

   b. *Set left*—He checks and releases, and goes directly to Dog-zone to pick up the first defensive back to come out of Baker-zone.

3. *Right tackle*—Blocks *inside gap-on-N.L.B.* in order of priority.

4. *Right guard*—Blocks inside *gap-on-N.L.B.* in order of priority.

5. *Center*—Blocks *outside gap-on-N.L.B.* in order of priority.

6. *Left guard*—Blocks *outside gap-on-N.L.B.* in order of priority.

7. *Left tackle*—Check and release to Charlie.

Odd calls (3 and 7 Powers) *are to the left* (Figure 2-6). Here are the rules as they are applied by each position:

  1. *Split end:*

    a. *Set left*—Apply mirror block.

    b. *Set right*—Check and release to short Baker.

  2. *Tight end:*

    a. *Set left*—Apply *inside gap-N.L.B.* on a 3 call; pulls and seals on a 7 call.

    b. *Set right*—Check and release to short Baker.

  3. *Left tackle:* Blocks *inside gap-on-N.L.B.* in order of priority.

  4. *Left guard:* Blocks *inside gap-on-N.L.B.* in order of priority.

  5. *Center:* Blocks *outside gap-on-N.L.B.* in order of priority.

  6. *Right Guard:* Blocks *outside gap-on-N.L.B.* in order of priority.

  7. *Right tackle:* Check and release to short Able.

The technique used in applying these basic power rules is to come out of a

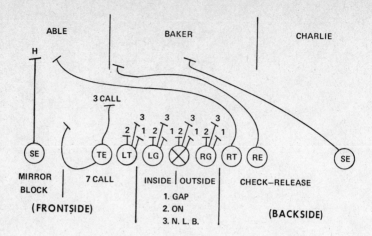

FIGURE 2-6: ODD POWER RULES, 3-7 CALLS

four point stance fast and low with head up. Make contact with your face in the numbers and keep your legs driving. If you begin to lose contact, slide your head and arms between the legs and keep driving on all fours. Never go to your knees. This is known as a scramble technique, and is to only be used as a secondary, desperation measure.

We never use 2 and 3 power calls in short-yardage situations. This is because short yardage defenses usually fill the gaps and the block is very difficult at the point-of-attack. In short yardage situations, we use our tandem and isolation plays.

TANDEM RULES

The word tandem means to double team at the point-of-attack. On a "tandem" call, the puller seals. On "trap" or "reverse" calls the puller traps. On "isolation" calls no one pulls. Outside of this the rules are the same.

We pull our guards on 4, 5, 6 and 7 calls, and we pull our tackles on 0, 1, 2 and 3 calls. Tandem rules are related to the singlewing type of blocking. We use every term except "reach" in the application of the tandem rules. The key to tandem blocking is the call man (Figure 2-4). Everyone should know where he is since he is the point-of-attack. The call man always has the lead block. The offensive lineman to his inside is the post man, and the lineman to his outside is the seal man. The whole team must be able to relate to these three men. The call man can take the split he needs to get clear of a defensive lineman on him.

EVEN TANDEM CALLS ARE TO THE RIGHT (Figure 2-7)

Here are the rules as they relate to the 4 call man: The 4 call man is the right tackle:

1. *Right tackle* lead blocks the first man on or off the line of scrimmage to his inside.
2. *Tight end* (set right) seals.

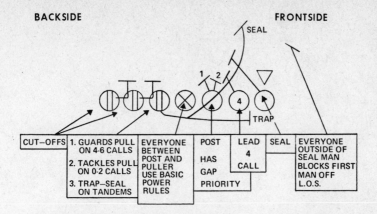

FIGURE 2-7: TANDEM RULES FOR EVEN CALLS

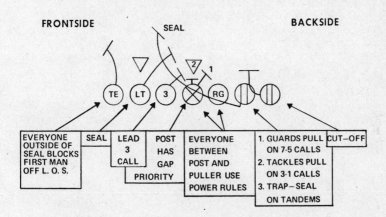

FIGURE 2-8: TANDEM RULES FOR ODD CALLS

3. *Right guard*—Inside gap priority, post.

4. *Center*—Outside gap-on-N.L.B.

5. *Left guard*—Pull and seal.

6. *Left tackle*—Cut off.

7. *Tight end*—(Set left) cut off.

8. *Split end*—Same as power rules.

ODD TANDEM CALLS ARE TO THE LEFT (Figure 2-8)

Here are the rules as they relate to the 3 call man. The 3 call man is the left guard.

1. *Left guard*—Lead block.

2. *Center*—Outside gap post.

3. *Left tackle*—Seal.

4. *Tight end*—(Set left) N.L.B.

5. *Right guard*—Outside gap-on-N.L.B.

6. *Right tackle*—Pull and seal.

7. *Tight end*—(Set right) cut-off.

8. *Split end*—Same as power rules.

Now we will apply our tandem rules and the variations at all points-of-attack (Figure 2-9). On 0, 1, 2 and 3 calls the center is always the lead man on even defenses and a guard is the lead man on odd defenses. These are the inside holes that we pull our tackles on. On these holes we usually set the tight end from the call.

1 tandem vs. 44-even defense (Figure 2-9a). The right guard and center (1 call man) post and lead. The left guard seals. The left tackle blocks the N.L.B. The right tackle pulls through the hole blocking the first man he sees. Notice the double team blocking angles at the point-of-attack.

2 tandem vs. 52 monster defense (Figure 2-9b). The center and right guard (2 call man) have the post and lead. The right tackle seals. The left guard uses his power rules. The left tackle pulls through the hole.

3 trap vs. 52 monster defense (Figure 2-9c). The only difference between this and a 1 or 3 tandem is that the right tackle pulls and traps the first defensive man to show to the left of center.

0 trap vs. 44 even defense (Figure 2-9d). The only difference between this and a 0 or 2 tandem is that the left tackle pulls and traps the first defensive man to show to the right of center.

Now let us apply our tandem rules to the inside and outside of tackles. They are the 4, 5, 6 and 7 calls. We pull our guards on off-tackle holes. On these wide holes we usually set the tight end to the call.

5 tandem vs. 44 even defense (Figure 2-9e). The left guard and the left tackle (5 call man) have the post and lead. The tight end seals. The center uses power rules. The right guard pulls through the hole. The right tackle uses the cut-off block.

4 tandem vs. 52 monster defense (Figure 2-9f). The right guard and the right tackle (4 call man) have the post and lead. Notice that against this defense they block the man off the line-of-scrimmage. The center applies his power rules. The left guard pulls through the hole, and the left tackle uses the cut-off block.

5 iso vs. 52 monster defense (Figure 2-9g). The only difference between an isolation and tandem is that no one pulls. Everyone from the post man (left guard) through the backside applies the power rules.

4 iso vs. 44 defense (Figure 2-9h). The only difference between this and a 4 tandem is that no one pulls. Everyone from the post man (right guard) through the backside applies the power rules.

7 tandem vs. 44 defense (Figure 2-9i). Since the tight end is the call man he always lines up to the call. The left tackle and tight end (7 call man) have the post and lead on the inside linebacker. The left guard and center apply their power rules. The right guard pulls through the hole and seals. The right tackle uses the cut-off block.

6 tandem vs. 52 monster defense (Figure 2-9j). The right tackle and tight

Figure 2-9a: 1 Tandem

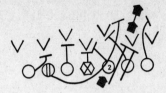

Figure 2-9b: 2 Tandem

Figure 2-9c: 3 Trap

Figure 2-9d: 0 Trap

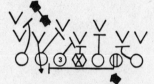

Figure 2-9e: 5 Tandem

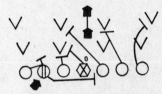

Figure 2-9f: 4 Tandem

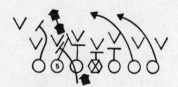

Figure 2-9g: 5 ISO

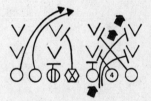

Figure 2-9h: 4 ISO

Figure 2-9i: 7 Tandem

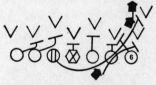

Figure 2-9j: 6 Tandem

ODD CALLS   **EVEN CALLS**

FIGURE 2-9: APPLICATION OF TANDEM RULES

end (6 call man) have the post and lead. The right guard and center apply their power rules. The left guard pulls through the hole and seals. The left tackle uses the cut-off block.

Tandem and isolation blocking is best to use in short yardage situations. It is because of the angles of the seal and lead blocks against gap defenses at the point-of-attack. You can block out on the outside gap of the hole. The post man has inside gap priority which most of the time will eliminate the double team block. The lead man still has a good angle to block him by himself.

SWEEP RULES

We combine trap and sweep techniques to get outside. We pull both guards. The frontside linemen basically need only three terms. They must use the following order of priorities: *reach, inside gap* and *inside linebacker*. The backside linemen use cut-off blocks.

EVEN SWEEP CALLS ARE TO THE RIGHT (Figure 2-10)

Here are the rules as they relate to each position:

1. *Wingback*—Blocks *reach-inside gap-I.L.B.* in order of priority.

2. *Tight end*—Blocks *reach-inside gap-I.L.B.* in order of priority.

3. *Right tackle*—Blocks *reach-inside gap-I.L.B.* in order of priority.

4. *Right guard* a. *4 call*—Pull and influence.

       b. *6 call*—Pull and trap.

       c. *8 call*—Pull and seal.

5. *Center*—Blocks *inside gap-on-outside gap-N.L.B.* in order of priority.

6. *Left guard* a. *4 call*—Pull and trap.

       b. *6 call*—Pull and seal.

       c. *8 call*—Pull and seal.

7. *Left tackle*—cut-off.

8. *Tight end*—(set right) cut-off.

9. *Split end*—Same as power rules.

ODD SWEEP CALLS ARE TO THE LEFT (Figure 2-11)

Here are the rules as they relate to each position:

1. *Wingback*—Blocks *reach-inside gap-I.L.B.* in order of priority.

2. *Tight end*—Blocks *reach-inside gap-I.L.B.* in order of priority.

3. *Left tackle*—Blocks *reach-inside gap-I.L.B.* in order of priority.

4. *Left guard* a. *4 call*—Pull and influence.

       b. *6 call*—Pull and trap.

       c. *8 call*—Pull and seal.

5. *Center*—Blocks *inside gap-on-outside gap-I.L.B.* in order of priority.

6. *Right guard* a. *4 call*—Pull and trap.

       b. *6 call*—Pull and seal.

       c. *8 call*—Pull and seal.

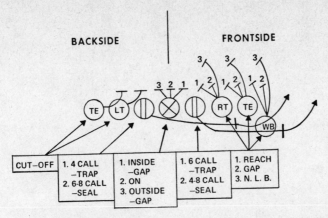

FIGURE 2-10: SWEEP RULES FOR EVEN CALLS

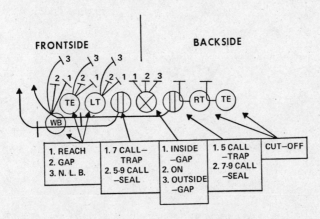

FIGURE 2-11: SWEEP RULES FOR ODD CALLS

7. *Right tackle*—Cut-off.

8. *Tight end*—(Set left) cut-off.

9. *Split end*—Same as power rules.

Now we will apply our sweep rules to 4-5-6-7-8-9 calls so we can see how some positions are affected by the variations (Figure 2-12).

5 sweep vs. 44 defense (Figure 2-12a). The left tackle is 5 call man and maintains his basic sweep rule. The tight end and wingback block the first men off the line of scrimmage since they are to the outside of call. The left guard influences widely. The right guard traps at the point-of-attack. All other positions maintain their basic sweep rules.

4 sweep vs. 52 monster defense (Figure 2-12b). The right tackle is the 4 call man and maintains his basic sweep rule. The tight end and wingback back block the first men off the line of scrimmage since they are to the outside of call. The

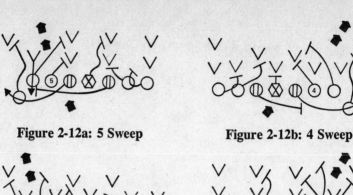

Figure 2-12a: 5 Sweep

Figure 2-12b: 4 Sweep

Figure 2-12c: 7 Sweep

Figure 2-12d: 6 Sweep

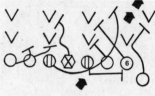

Figure 2-12e: 9 Sweep

Figure 2-12f: 8 Sweep

ODD CALLS

EVEN CALLS

FIGURE 2-12: APPLICATION OF SWEEP RULES

right guard influences widely. The left guard traps at the point-of-attack. All remaining positions apply their basic sweep rules.

7 sweep vs. 52 monster (Figure 2-12c). The tight end is the 7 call man. The wingback blocks the first man off the line of scrimmage since he is to the outside of call. Left guard pulls and traps. Right guard pulls and seals. All remaining positions apply their basic sweep rules.

6 sweep vs. 44 defense (Figure 2-12d). The tight end is the 6 call man. The wingback blocks the first man off the line of scrimmage since he is to the outside of the call. The right guard pulls and traps. The left guard pulls and seals. All remaining positions apply their basic sweep rules.

9 sweep vs. 44 defense (Figure 2-12e). The wingback is the 9 call man. The left guard pulls and blocks the first outside man off the line of scrimmage. All remaining positions apply their basic sweep rules.

8 sweep vs. 52 monster defense (Figure 2-12f). The wingback is the 8 call man. The right guard pulls and blocks the first outside man off the line of scrimmage. All remaining positions apply their basic sweep rules.

On 8 and 9 sweeps only, about 20 percent of sweeps get around the corner. The remaining 80 percent of sweeps cut back head on into the pursuit.

RELATING TO THE CALLS

Over the years these blocking rules have held up. The only breakdown was on a split 6 defense. We solved this by switching the guards' and tackles' responsibilities. We have been able to apply these three sets of blocking rules to 48 formations without breakdowns. Now that we have covered *power, tandem* and *sweep* rules, we will cover the three backfield techniques to go with them. They will have the same names so we can integrate the right backfield technique with the correct blocking rule.

CHAPTER 3

Coaching the Multiple Power "I" Backfield Techniques

The backfield patterns and sets vary from time to time. When you add a new sequence to your system or experiment with new plays, these start in the backfield. If some fit into your system, you can naturally co-ordinate them with your blocking schemes.

Over the past years our backfield patterns and sets have changed drastically, while our blocking schemes have remained basically the same. This alone should express the merit of our blocking rules. We have graduated from the singlewing and short punt to the split "T," to the wing "T," and have arrived at the fullhouse "I" set. Today we could take any of those basic patterns and sequences from past formations and successfully co-ordinate it behind our blocking scheme. The arrival at a power "I" backfield set has been the result of gradual step-by-step improvements. We feel the positions within the set itself are more variable and protect us against weak tendencies. In certain situations, if we feel our fullhouse "I" set is a liability to our tactical pattern, we can shift out of it —usually back to one of our old wing "T" formations. Our fullhouse "I" set is home base, and regardless of what set we are in, we would not feel secure without a man in the fullback position.

We use three basic running techniques for our backs. They are *power*, *tandem* and *sweep* techniques. The power techniques are applied to our fullback ride and option plays. The tandem techniques feature the tailback running behind double team blocking. The sweep techniques include fake sweep actions with the use of slants and reverses.

Our basic power "I" backfield set has the following advantages:

1. We can flip-flop our wingback and still place balance pressure on both sides of the set by using tandem techniques to the wingback's side and power option techniques to the backside (Figure 3-1).

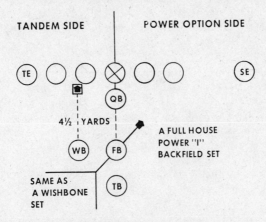

FIGURE 3-1: BASIC BACKFIELD SET

2. We can also run our power techniques to the frontside of the set.
3. Our tandem techniques can be perfected and made effective in a limited amount of time. This provides the time that is needed to work on our power option techniques (Figure 3-1).
4. A full-house power "I" backfield set is basically the same as a wishbone set. (Figure 3-1)
5. All we have to do is flip-flop our wingback to change to the tandem side (Figure 3-2).

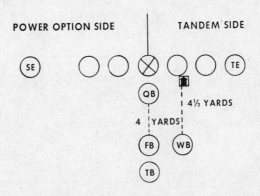

FIGURE 3-2: FLIP-FLOP THE WINGBACK

6. The power "I" set is the best formation for the deployment of personnel to another set using the shift.

The fullback lines up 4 yards behind the quarterback in a three-point stance. The wingback lines up 4½ yards behind the outside heel of the guard in a three-point stance. This is his halfback set. The tailback lines up one yard behind the fullback in a three-point stance. Most tailbacks are in a two-point stance so he can read the block. Our tailback knows where he is going before the set or snap.

RELATING TO SERIES

The first of two digits used in calling the plays indicated the series. The series will tell the backfield from what set they will run their basic techniques. We can use nine series in our calls. This is the multiple aspect of the offense and will be covered in Chapter 4. It is important that we relate the technique to the series. Each technique has a backfield pattern; each back's pattern covers certain holes. If his holes are called, he gets the ball. If other holes are called, he carries out his pattern without the ball. In the tandem techniques the series can determine the backs' blocking or running assignments. This is because there is no backfield pattern, and the techniques call for blocking from the backs who are not carrying the ball.

POWER TECHNIQUES

Our power techniques are the same as those of triple option, except that we predetermine our hand-off to the fullback and only option off the defensive end. In the power backfield pattern the quarterback lead steps and rides the fullback to the outside heel of the guard. The quarterback then continues down the line of scrimmage and tries to pitch to the backside back. The frontside back leads wide. For this we only need two holes to run the pattern. We call 2 power and 6 power to the right, and 3 power and 7 power to the left.

2 power techniques (Figure 3-3). We give the ball to the fullback over the right guard. Before the snap the fullback checks to see if there is a defensive lineman in the gap between right guard and tackle. If a man is in the gap he will slide to the outside. If no man is in the gap, he will drive directly through the gap. Predetermining this during the set eliminates any hesitation after the snap. On the snap the fullback explodes from his set with his left arm parallel to eye level and runs directly to the outside heel of the guard (Figure 3-3). The quarterback will

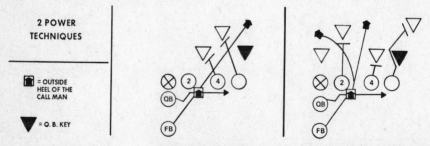

2 POWER
TECHNIQUES

■ = OUTSIDE
HEEL OF THE
CALL MAN

▼ = Q. B. KEY

Figure 3-3a: Gap   Figure 3-3b: Uncovered

FIGURE 3-3

lead step, put the ball in fullback's numbers, and ride him to heel of guard. This is where the fullback receives full control of the ball. Only after this does he slide to outside of the gap (Figure 3-3a) or blast through the gap (Figure 3-3b) as predetermined. As soon as the quarterback has handed the ball off he keys the defensive end for a possible pitch on the next play.

3 power techniques (Figure 3-4). This is the same as 2 power to the left. We will go through this play in order of development.

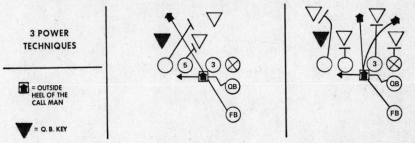

3 POWER
TECHNIQUES

▪ = OUTSIDE
HEEL OF THE
CALL MAN

▼ = Q. B. KEY

Figure 3-4a: Gap   **Figure 3-4b: Uncovered**

FIGURE 3-4

1. On the set the fullback checks gap (Figures 3-4a and 3-4b).
2. On the snap the fullback drives to outside heel of left guard with right arm up.
3. The quarterback lead steps and puts ball in the fullback's numbers. He rides to the guard's left heel.
4. The fullback closes down on the ball and slides to the outside gap (Figure 3-4a) or through the gap (Figure 3-4b).
5. The quarterback checks the defensive end for a future call.
6. The tight end blocks off the line of scrimmage.

6 power techniques (Figure 3-5a). After running the 2 power the quarterback notices that the defensive end is closing down. After faking to the fullback he keys the end and pitches to the tailback. Notice that the tailback has both the

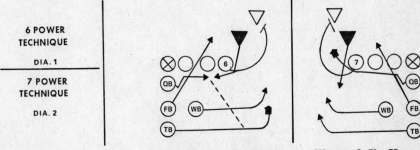

6 POWER
TECHNIQUE

DIA. 1

7 POWER
TECHNIQUE

DIA. 2

Figure 3-5a: Pitchout   **Figure 3-5b: Keeper**

FIGURE 3-5

wingback as a lead back out of the backfield and the tight end in front of him. This is a very high-risk play and is to be used sparingly for big yardage.

7 power techniques (Figure 3-5b). On this play we are trying to get the pitch out, but the defensive end is in the area so the quarterback is forced to keep. It is still possible for him to lateral after he gets past the line of scrimmage.

TANDEM TECHNIQUES

The most important thing for both the runners and blockers in the backfield to know is the spot at the outside heel of the post man (Figure 3-6). This will

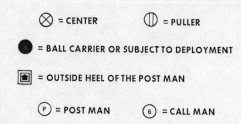

FIGURE 3-6: SYMBOL KEYS FOR TANDEM TECHNIQUES

always be the first man to the inside of the call. If the blocker goes full speed to that spot and turns out, he cannot help but make his proper block; if the ball carrier goes full speed to that spot he can't miss the hole. Here we will make the call and relate it to the post man's outside heel;

1. *7 tandem*—Left tackle is post man (left heel).
2. *5 tandem*—Left guard is post man (left heel).
3. *4 tandem*—Right guard is post man (right heel).
4. *6 tandem*—Right tackle is post man (right heel).

Our tandem techniques have no backfield patterns or faking as in sweep or power techniques. Because of this, the series indicates the ball carrier. The tailback gets the ball on 50 and 60 series, the fullback gets the ball on 30 and 90 series, and the wingback gets the ball on 70 and 80 series. These assignments will be discussed in Chapter 7-8.

In our tandem techniques the quarterback always uses a reverse pivot on the

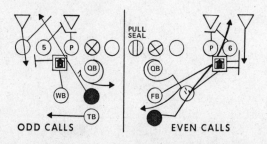

FIGURE 3-7: TANDEM TECHNIQUES

snap. After he hands off, he bootlegs back away from the call (Figure 3-7). On the odd 5 call the wingback goes to the outside heel of the left guard (Figure 3-7). If he does this before he turns out, he can't miss his block. The fullback takes the ball running through the same hole. This is an example of an isolation play. On the even 6 call the right tackle is the post man. His outside heel is the spot. The fullback and wingback go to that spot before they tandem out. The tailback takes the ball through that spot (Figure 3-7).

SWEEP TECHNIQUES

Our sweep techniques integrate a slant technique and the inside reverse. The quarterback always lead steps on all sweep techniques.

The wingback always shifts from his halfback position to a flanker set on all sweep techniques. He sets to the call and has the following blocking and running assignments (Figure 3-8):

1. On 8 and 9 sweep calls he uses the frontside sweep blocking rules: *reach-inside gap-N.L.B.*

2. On the 4, 5, 6 and 7 sweep calls a slant technique is used. He blocks the first man off the line of scrimmage to his inside.

3. On a 0 or 1 reverse calls he sets as a backside flanker and takes the ball on an inside hand-off.

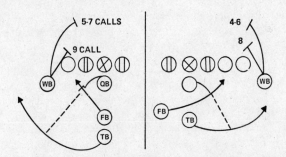

FIGURE 3-8: SWEEP-SLANT TECHNIQUES

Now we will examine the sweep-slant backfield action. It is a two-play sequence, with the tailback taking the ball on the first play and the fullback taking it on the second play. Regardless of the set, the tailback gets the pitch out on an 8 or 9 sweep call, and the fullback gets the ball running a slant pattern on a 4, 5, 6 or 7 sweep calls (Figure 3-8). After the quarterback has pitched on the 8 or 9 sweep calls, his hands remain extended and the fullback fakes by covering over his extended hands. On the 4, 5, 6 or 7 hole the quarterback fakes the pitchout and leaves the ball extended for the fullback to take the hand-off on a slant into the hole that is called. This is a very simple technique to teach which is also very deceptive. Here it is important to add that basically we use the sweep with the fullback leading the play out of the backfield. Figure 3-8a shows the sweep-slant technique used with a 9 and 5 call; Figure 3-8b shows the sweep-slant technique used with an 8 and 6 call.

In the reverse the quarterback lead steps out, fakes a pitchout to the tailback,

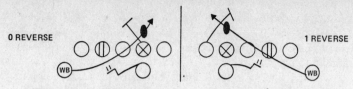

Figure 3-9a: 0 Reverse   Figure 3-9b: 1 Reverse

FIGURE 3-9: REVERSE (FAKE SWEEP) TECHNIQUES

and gives an inside hand-off to the wingback up the middle (Figure 3-9). The wingback sets as a flanker from the call. On the snap he takes a direct path to where the ball was set. "Reverse" is a "trap" synonym. The tackle pulls and traps. This is very effective after running a number of successful sweeps.

RECOGNIZING THE DEFENSIVE HOLE

All defenses have weaknesses for a point-of-attack; different defenses leave different weaknesses. It is very important to recognize the best holes to run. This eliminates guessing, wasting plays and inconsistency. The quarterback must learn to recognize defenses and know what to call. The ball carrier must learn to recognize where the daylight is at the point-of-attack before the snap so there will be no hesitation after the snap. We try to attack two kinds of situations at a point-of-attack. They are the outside gaps and uncovered call men. An uncovered call man has no down defensive lineman on him. We can use three popular defenses used today to cover almost any situation (Figure 3-10). The strengths and weaknesses of these three defenses are:

1. *44 stack* (Figure 3-10a). This defense is usually a stunting type of defense. It has four doubles that could work independently of one another filling inside and outside gaps. It leaves our center and tackles uncovered. The uncovered center is deceiving. There are four men on three. They can gap out with their guards and fill the inside gaps with the inside linebacker before we can get a fourth man there. The uncovered tackle situation is different. We can get our fourth man there before they do, and they leave us a lot of running room. Our guards and center close down splits and wedge at 1-0. We attack the 4-5-8-9 holes with our quick direct plays. They may get us a few times, but in return we are going to break some big ones on them. The angle of our uncovered tackle and the release of our tight end are to our advantage. Their outside stunts will get them in trouble since our fourth man is more concerned about getting to a spot where he has the advantage than about who he is to block. We have had consistent success against 44 defenses. Our blocking rules have taken care of us without breakdowns.

2. *52 monster* (Figure 3-10b). This defense is usually a technique type of defense. It is basically the same as the old Oklahoma 54. We like to attack it with our tandem offense at the 2-3 uncovered holes and the 6-7 hole gaps. A 4-5 sweep-slant technique can be very effective if our guard can influence their inside linebacker out of the hole. We like to pick up the monster's tendencies and run away from him. If we can't do this, we consider him the same as a corner back on an Oklahoma 54.

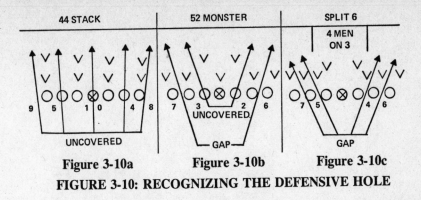

| 44 STACK | 52 MONSTER | SPLIT 6 |

Figure 3-10a   Figure 3-10b   Figure 3-10c

FIGURE 3-10: RECOGNIZING THE DEFENSIVE HOLE

3. *Split 6* (Figure 3-10c). This defense is usually a technique type defense. It presents the same four on three situation for our uncovered center as the 44 stack defense, but the problem it causes is very different. Almost everyone's blocking rules have had to have an adjustment made in this situation. The guard's rules usually put him on the linebacker. He can't get to him because of the reach technique used by their defensive down lineman. This left the linebackers free. Don't ever get caught unprepared for this situation or you could be in big trouble. We like to run at all the gaps to the outside of our guards with tandems, isolations and sweeps. We treat it with the same approach we would use on an 8 gap defense.

By now you should be able to make the following relationships between our backfield techniques and blocking rules:

1. With power techniques we use power blocking rules.
2. With tandem, isolation and reverse techniques we use tandem blocking rules.
3. With sweep and slant techniques we use sweep blocking rules.
4. Isolation blocking is a halfbreed between power and tandem rules. We use tandem rules from the call man to the frontside, and power rules from the post man to the backside.
5. The reverse is used with a sweep backfield technique and tandem (trap) blocking rules.
6. The ball carriers in power and sweep backfield patterns are determined by the holes that are called out of their sequences.
7. The ball carrier in the tandem techniques is determined by the number of the series that is called.

Before we can coordinate our backfield and line into team application, we need to understand the method or system for getting multiple sets. The multiple sets in the line will be determined in the huddle, and they go directly to those positions on the break. The offensive backs will break to their power "I" set, and then shift to their multiple sets. The following chapter will explain our multiple system.

CHAPTER 4

Splitting the Series to Get Multiple Power "I" Sets

We have seen many methods used to obtain multiple formations: some of them are good; others were not. There are a couple of things that all the good methods have in common: they have a good set of blocking rules and call their sets in series. This does not mean you can not number your backs and still have a good multiple system. An example of a good method that we know is to add a third digit before the call such as 100, 200, 300, etc., to indicate the formation. You can have nine sets and still number your backs, but you are still calling in series.

Our system for a multiple offense has been with us since the integration of our blocking rules, but there have been some modifications since then. Our multiple system has been as effective as it has been different. We only change our sets with a purpose in mind. Thirty of our 48 formations basically only affect the positions of three offensive men. Because we are so involved in the deployment of these men with a goal in mind, we do not worry about what formations we are in. Football scouts on the outside realize this. Sometimes we show a lot of formations while looking for an advantage; other times we set in one formation and stay with it as long as we have an advantage. Outsiders' viewpoints are very different from ours: they view the total formation with concern. We don't worry about the complete formation we are in, concentrating only on how the defense responds to the deployment of our three offensive men and how we can take advantage of their defensive sets. We have run into a lot of situations. Some of them have been surprising. We have seen undershifts, overshifts, gaps and some confused defenses. What surprises us the most is when we gain a definite advantage and the defense does not adjust. If they are not going to adjust, we are not going to change.

SPLITTING SERIES

There are two ways to split the series. One is to split odd and even series to get sets in our line, and the second is to use the upper and lower series to determine the frontside or backside of the backfield. This effects the deployment of three positions: the tight end, split end and wingback. The individual series determines the formation and shift that are to be used for deployment.

ODD AND EVEN SERIES

The side of the line that the tight end sets to in relation to the call is determined by whether it is an odd or even series. On odd series the tight end lines up to the call side; on even series he lines up from the call (Figure 4-1). In course an odd or even hole determines the side of the call. Any even series is the same as any odd series that it follows. The backfield techniques and sets will be the same in both of these series; for example, 10 and 20 series will feature the same plays, as will the 70 and 80 series. Occasionally we will add a 100 series to go with the 90 series. We have never had a tight end who has had any problems in learning to do this. He must be a good blocker on odd series calls; on even series calls he will either have the cut-off or check-release.

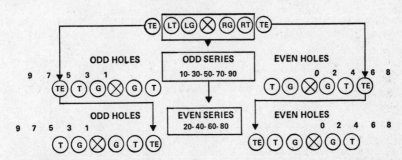

FIGURE 4-1: TIGHT END'S SET FOR ODD AND EVEN SERIES

GETTING BALANCED AND UNBALANCED LINES

The split end's calls are simply "split left" or "split right." His set will determine if there is a balanced or unbalanced line. We get our line set through a combination of flip-flopping our split end with our tight end. A game plan sometimes predetermines the split end's set by applying the same method as the tight end on odd and even hold calls (Figure 4-2). Most of the time we just call it in the huddle.

Balanced lines are obtained by setting the split end left or right with the following relationships and results:

1. On even series and odd hole calls we set the split end to the left. This results in a slot to the left (Figure 4-2).

2. On odd series and even hole calls we set the split end to the left. This results in a flanker to the right (Figure 4-2).

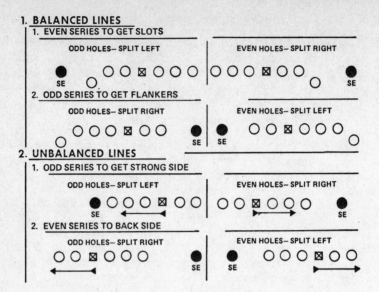

FIGURE 4-2: SPLIT END CALLS FOR LINE SETS

3. On even series and even hole calls we set the split end to the right. This results in a slot to the right (Figure 4-2).

4. On odd series and odd hole calls we set the split end to the right. This results in a flanker to the left (Figure 4-2).

A simple conclusion for getting balanced lines is to set the split end from the call on odd series and set him to the call on even series.

Unbalanced lines are obtained by setting the split end left or right with the following relationships and results:

1. On odd series and odd hole calls we set the split end to the left. This results in running the play to the strongside left of an unbalanced line (Figure 4-2).

2. On even series and even hole calls we set the split end to the left. This results in running the play to the shortside right of an unbalanced line (Figure 4-2).

3. On odd series and even hole calls we set the split end to the right. This results in running the play to the strongside right of an unbalanced line (Figure 4-2).

4. On even series and odd hole calls we set the split end right. This results in running the play to the short side left of an unbalanced line (Figure 4-2).

A simple conclusion for getting unbalanced lines is to set the split end to the call on odd series and to set him from the call on even series.

When you are not accustomed to making these relationships they may seem difficult or confusing, but when you put them into actual application they become very simple. They provide 8 different line sets. Now we will study the method of getting multiple backfield sets to go with them.

USING FRONTSIDE AND BACKSIDE SERIES

The side on which the wingback is set is termed the frontside and the side away from him is termed the backside. On the lower (10-20-30-40-50-60) frontside series the wingback sets to call. On the upper (70-80-90 and all reverses) backside series the wingback sets from the call. The techniques and shift of the 90 series are the same as the 10 and 20 frontside series to the backside. The 70 and 80 backside series have the same techniques as the 30 and 40 frontside series. Now we will put our two methods of splitting series together and relate them through application.

MULTIPLE FORMATIONS

No more than half of our possible 48 formations could be considered practical. We will examine only those sets that have been in our repertory during recent years and will illustrate 30 formations.

First in our 10 and 20 series we use primarily the sweep-slant techniques (Figure 4-3). To get the same 10 and 20 backfield formation and techniques to the backside we use the 90 series call.

1. *Figures 4-3a and 4-3b* show the shifts from the power "I" set to the 10-20 backfield sets. The wing back shifts from his halfback sets to the flanker positions to his side. The fullback shifts from the call to a halfback set and the tailback shifts forward into his position.

   (Figure 4-3a) shows the odd hole call shift to the left on 10 and 20 series. On 90 even calls you get the same shift from the call.

   (Figure 4-3b) shows the even hold call shift to the right on 10 and 20 series. On 90 odd calls you get the same shift from the call.

2. *Figures 4-3c and 4-3d.* With the 10 series, if you set the split end from the call you will get a floater set with a flanker behind a balanced line. Occasionally, to get the same backside set, we would use a 100 series.

   (Figure 4-3c) shows the odd hole calls with a flanker left and a balanced line.

   (Figure 4-3d) shows the even hole calls with a flanker right and a balanced line.

3. *Figures 4-3e and 4-3f.* With the *10 series*, if you set the split end to the call you will get a floater slot backfield set to the strongside of an unbalanced line. Again, you would have to use the 100 series to get the same formation for the backside.

   (Figure 4-3e) shows the odd hole calls with a slot set left to the strongside of an unbalanced line.

   (Figure 4-3f) shows the even hole calls with a slot set right to the strongside of an unbalanced line.

4. *Figures 4-3g and 4-3h.* With the *20 series* if you set the split end to the call you will get a slot set to the call on a balanced line. To get this same set for a backside play you will call a 90 series with the split end set from the call.

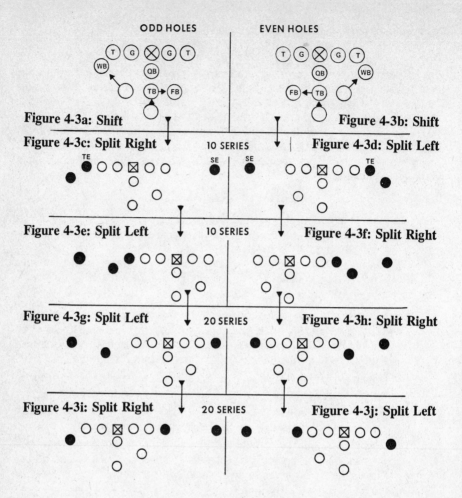

FIGURE 4-3: MULTIPLE SETS FOR 10-20 SERIES

(Figure 4-3g) shows the odd hole calls with a slot set left behind a balanced line.

(Figure 4-3h) shows the even hole calls with a slot set right behind a balanced line.

5. *Figures 4-3i and 4-3j.* With the *20 series*, if you set the split end from the call we will get a flanker to the shortside of an unbalanced line. To get the same set for a backside play you will call a 90 series with the split end set to the call.

(Figure 4-3i) shows the odd hole calls with a flanker set left to the shortside of an unbalanced line.

(Figure 4-3j) shows the even hole calls with a flanker set right to the shortside of an unbalanced line.

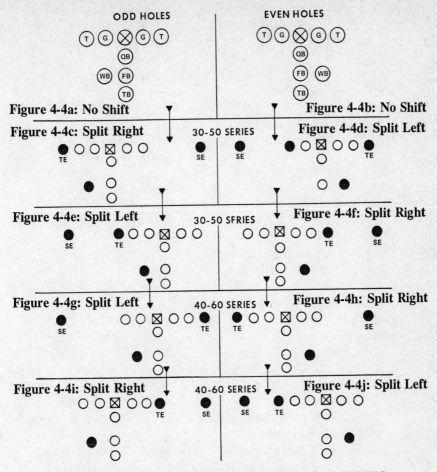

FIGURE 4-4: MULTIPLE SETS FOR 30-40-50-60 SERIES

On any even series call we can not make 6 or 7 tandem and sweep calls because the 6 and 7 call man (tight end) is set from the call. We can make 6 or 7 power calls. The combination of these two backfield sets and four line sets gives us a total of eight formations.

With the 30, 40, 50 and 60 series we maintain a fullhouse "I" backfield set without a shift (Figure 4-4). With the 30 and 40 series we basically use our power techniques to the wingback side. In running these power techniques to the backside (from the wingback) we use 70 and 80 series calls. We use 50 and 60 series calls for the tandem and isolation techniques.

   1. *Figures 4-4a and 4-4b* show the wingback set in a halfback position to the call in a full house backfield set without a shift. In a backside series the halfback would be set from the call.

   (Figure 4-4a) shows the wingback set left on an odd hole call.

(Figure 4-4b) shows the wingback set right on an even hole call.

2. *Figures 4-4c and 4-4d*. With *30 and 50 series*, if you set the split end from the call you will have the wingback set in a halfback position to the tight side of a balanced line.

(Figure 4-4c) shows the wingback set left on an odd hole call to the tight side of a balanced line.

(Figure 4-4d) shows the wingback set right on an even hole call to the tight side of a balanced line.

3. *Figures 4-4e and 4-4f*. With *30 and 50 series*, if you set the split end to the call you will have the wingback set in a halfback position to the strongside of an unbalanced line.

(Figure 4-4e) shows the wingback set left on an odd hole call to the strongside of an unbalanced line.

(Figure 4-4f) shows the wingback set right on an even hole call to the strongside of an unbalanced line.

4. *Figures 4-4g and 4-4h*. With *40 and 60 series*, if you set the split end to the call you will have the wingback set in a halfback position to the split side of a balanced line.

(Figure 4-4g) shows the wingback set left on an odd hold call to the split side of a balanced line.

(Figure 4-4h) shows the wingback set right on an even hold call to the split side of a balanced line.

5. *Figures 4-4i and 4-4j*. With *40 and 60 series*, if you set the split end from the call you will have the wingback set in a halfback position to the shortside of an unbalanced line.

(Figure 4-4i) shows the wingback set left on an odd hole call to the shortside of an unbalanced line.

(Figure 4-4j) shows the wingback set right on an even hole call to the shortside of an unbalanced line.

This now increases our number of sets to 16 formations.

With the 50 and 60 sweep series we always shift the wingback from his halfback set to the flanker set on the call side (Figure 4-5).

1. *Figures 4-5a and 4-5b* show the shifts of the wingback to his flanker sets.

(Figure 4-5a) shows the wingback shift left on odd hole calls.

(Figure 4-5b) shows the wingback shift right on even hole calls.

2. *Figure 4-5c and 4-5d*. With the *50 sweep series*, if you set the split end from the call you will have the wingback shift to a flanker set of a balanced line.

(Figure 4-5c) shows a flanker set left on an odd hole call to the tight side of a balanced line.

(Figure 4-5d) shows a flanker set right on an even hold call to the tight side of a balanced line.

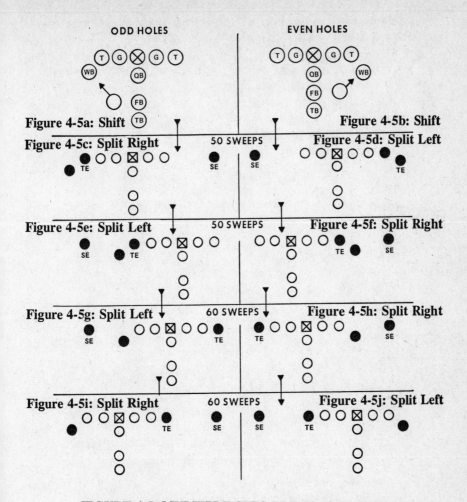

FIGURE 4-5: MULTIPLE SETS FOR 50-60 SWEEPS

3. *Figures 4-5e and 4-5f.* With the *50 sweep series*, if you set the split end to the call you will have the wingback shift to a slot set to the strongside of an unbalanced line.

   (Figure 4-5e) shows a slot set left on an odd hole call to the strongside of an unbalanced line.

   (Figure 4-5f) shows a slot set right on an even hole call to the strongside of an unbalanced line.

4. *Figures 4-5g and 4-5h.* With the *60 sweep series*, if you set the split end to the call you will have the wingback shift to a slot position of a balanced line.

   (Figure 4-5g) shows a slot set left on an odd call hole to the split side of a balanced line.

(Figure 4-5h) shows a slot set right on an even call hole to the split side of a balanced line.

5. *Figures 4-5i and 4-5j.* With the *60 sweep series*, if you set the split end from the call you will have the wingback shift to a flanker set to the shortside of an unbalanced line.

(Figure 4-5i) shows a flanker set left on an odd hole call to the shortside of an unbalanced line.

(Figure 4-5j) shows a flanker set right on an even hole call to the shortside of an unbalanced line.

We have now multiplied the number of sets so we have a total of 24 formations.

Using two tight ends in a short yardage situation and two split ends in a passing situation (Figure 4-6).

1. *Figures 4-6a and 4-6b.* We can put two split ends in the game with our quick draw offense. This gives a floater slot to the frontside and a split to the backside.

(Figure 4-6a.) We have a floater slot left.

(Figure 4-6b.) We have a floater slot right.

2. *Figures 4-6c, 4-6d, 4-6e and 4-6f.* We can put two tight ends in a short yardage situation and use them in both with balanced and unbalanced lines.

(Figure 4-6c.) We have our tandem set left on an odd hole call to the strongside of an unbalanced line.

(Figure 4-6d.) We have our tandem set right on an even hole call to the strongside of an unbalanced line.

(Figure 4-6e.) We have our tandem set left behind a balanced line.

(Figure 4-6f.) We have our tandem set right behind a balanced line.

This gives us a total of 30 formations.

APPLYING MULTIPLE FORMATIONS

The secret of a multiple offense is to take advantage of it in application. It can be misused and work against you if you make calls without a purpose in mind. Don't outsmart yourself! With multiple sets you can either shift them out of position and hit where they are not, or shift yourself into a position to your advantage. Before you can do this you must be able to very rapidly find what will work best for you and stay with it until the situation changes. When the situation changes you must be able to recognize this and change accordingly.

Once, when playing very formidable opponents, we found a weakness to which they never adjusted all night. We ran the same play 36 times with an average of seven-plus yards per try. We did not change the set, but we were forced to switch personnel to give the ball carrier a rest. The next year we ran the same play and set only during the first series. This time our opponents were ready for us and forced us to multiple application.

There are basically two approaches to defensing multiple sets. They are

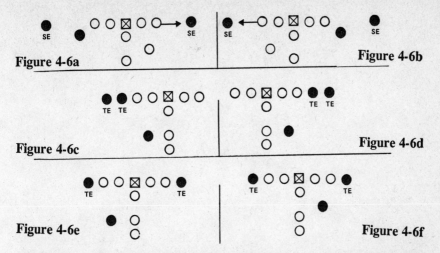

Figure 4-6a

Figure 4-6b

Figure 4-6c

Figure 4-6d

Figure 4-6e

Figure 4-6f

FIGURE 4-6: MULTIPLE SETS FOR QUICK DRAW-SHORT YARDAGE

either undershifted or overshifted defenses. The more common undershifted defense is one that rotates or adjusts with just a few men. In the overshift, the whole defensive front will shift down with you a full man. We very seldom see an overshift, but when we do, this is the only time we set our quarterback free in his calls. We mix the sets up and go on quick snaps. We want our opponents thinking, hesitating, confused and frustrated. We like to use personnel tendencies and tactical plans from scouting reports to determine the sets to our advantage —but very often the unexpected will happen.

READING THE DEFENSE

We need a method for quick adjustments to the unexpected, and must be able to read the defense immediately and find a new set to our advantage. In doing this we view all undershifted defenses as having the following common characteristics before the snap:

1. They all have 11 men. The odd number forces at least one man to have responsibilities to both sides. He could be either up front or in the secondary.

2. They all have two defensive halfbacks who flank their secondary and can be isolated regardless of their zone, man-to-man or outside rotating coverage. This reduces our concerns to the set of nine men.

3. We consider that all defenses have eight-man fronts with four men to the left, and four men to the right of center. We do not count corner backs. This leaves us with two men to be concerned with. These are the *fifth men* in the defensive set. There should be a fifth man to our left (odd) side and another to our right (even) side. If they are not, we want to know about it.

We assign two of our men to key areas to each side to locate their positions

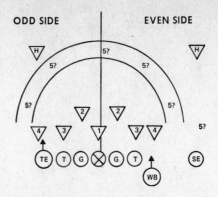

FIGURE 4-7: READING THE DEFENSE TO DETERMINE THE SET

before the snap and responsibilities after the snap. They are our tight end and wingback (Figure 4-7). We lead with a basic slot right balanced line. This is the best set we know to key areas.

The tight end keys the odd (left) side. This is an area between the defensive end, the defensive half, the middle deep spot and the hook spot. Any man in this area is the fifth man (Figure 4-7). Here are the keys of the tight end:

1. If there is a *fifth man* positioned off the line of scrimmage to the outside of the defensive end, he is the corner back or monster. Since most of the blocks by the tight end are off the line of scrimmage it should not take long to realize what his responsibilities are after the snap.

2. If there is a *fifth man* set in the hook area, he is either an invert or is covering the tight end in man-to-man coverage. The first time the call is away from the tight end he can leave down field on the snap as if running a pass pattern and very quickly determine what his responsibilities are after the snap.

3. If there is a *fifth man* set middle deep he is either a safety in zone coverage or a pre-rotated invert. In either case his responsibilities are basically the same.

4. If there is no *fifth man* in the odd (left) side area, we will assume that he has become the sixth man in the even (right) side area. If this is the case, we want to know about it in a hurry and attack that backside area with the proper sets.

The wingback has the same keys to the right (even) side. In addition, he needs to also look for the *fifth man* to be on the line of scrimmage as a force man, or on the split end for double coverage. If this is the situation, we will attack to the inside of them to the split side. This is because we have two of their men isolated as a result of our split end.

Since we are a specialized platoon team, we can plot these tendencies on a blackboard while the defense is on the field. We check ourself with the press box communication, and when the offense takes the field again we will have arrived at our new plan of attack.

MAKING SET ADJUSTMENTS

Now that we have established a method for reading the defense we will put it into application. We will show the following examples of making set adjustments to our advantage as a result of reading the defense.

1. *After starting out with a lead set, our tight end and wingback discover the defense is in a 52 monster* (Figure 4-8). The *fifth man's* set to our right is the monster. The *fifth man's* set to our left is in the safety position. Now we must check their responsibilities. The tight end soon learns that the safety is in zone coverage. Our wingback discovers the monster is keying the wingback. This means we can move our split end without any adjustment on the part of the monster. The adjustment we can make to our advantage is to set the split end to the call on the 70 power and 90 sweep series. This will give us a good backside attack to the strongside of an unbalanced line. To keep them honest we will mix in an occasional 60 tandem series with split end set from the call.

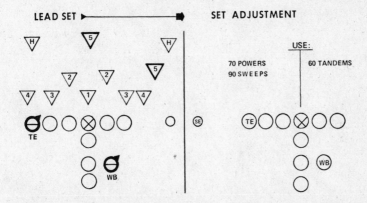

FIGURE 4-8: SET ADJUSTMENT FOR 52 MONSTER DEFENSE

2. *After starting out with a lead set we discover that they are in a 44 stack defense* (Figure 4-9). Our tight end and wingback soon learn that there are three *fifth men* in zone coverage. They are the safety and two corner backs. The only adjustment that is made in their pre-snap set is that the corner back to our right triangles our split. This means we can move our wingback to the opposite side without them making a set adjustment. We will set our wingback to the frontside of odd series calls and set our split end from the calls. We will keep them honest to our backside by mixing in the 20 power sequence with our split end set to the call. Keep in mind we can flip-flop this same plan of attack and run it to both sides.

3. *After starting out in a lead set, our tight end and wingback discover that the defense is in a pre-rotated invert* (Figure 4-10). The tight end discovers that the safety is keying our wingback man-to-man. Our wingback discovers the fifth man invert to his side is favoring the split end side. There is no reason to change the set since we already have an

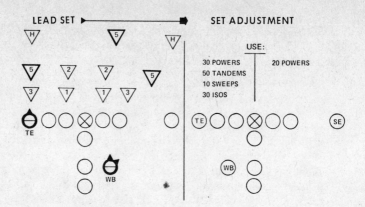

FIGURE 4-9: SET ADJUSTMENT FOR 44 STACK DEFENSE

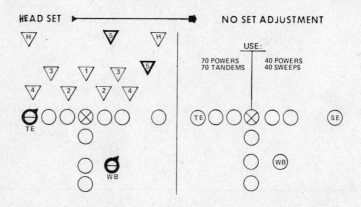

FIGURE 4-10: SET ADJUSTMENT FOR 43 INVERT DEFENSE

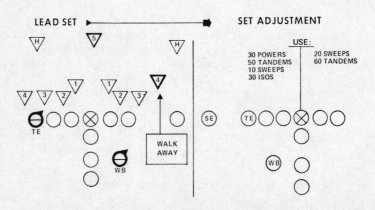

FIGURE 4-11: SET ADJUSTMENT FOR 62 SPLIT DEFENSE

advantage. We will use the 70 power and tandem series to our backside with the split end set from the call. Don't ever change a set when you already have an advantage, or you will be defeating the purpose of a multiple offense.

4. *Against a 62 split defense we find they can only adjust with a walk-away end to the split side of a balanced line* (Figure 4-11). We can set both our split end and wingback to the tight end's side and overload it. We will run the 30 powers, 50 tandems, 10 sweeps, and 30 isolations to the strongside of an unbalanced line in our frontside attack. To keep them honest we will occasionally mix in 20 sweeps and 60 tandems to the shortside of our unbalanced in our backside attack.

A general and simple concept of this method of reading defenses and making set adjustment to our advantage is that we are outpositioning two of their men with three of ours. It is a three on two concept. We can always position one of our three men where they don't have one. It is our tight end, split end and wingback vs. their two fifth men.

INTERCHANGING THE SERIES TO FIT THE TIMES

We have covered only 30 of the 48 possible formations, but these are more than enough. A change in time and personnel can prompt a revival of one of our old series to replace a present series. This also is a check for us not having too much offense and working on things we do not need. If we don't use them, we don't need them.

The *bifocal pattern* is an excellent example of one of our mothball series we keep subject to recall (Figure 4-12). It is natural to shift the whole backfield from a power "I" set to the strongside of an unbalanced line. The tailback shifts to a halfback set, the fullback shifts to a blocking back position, and the wingback shifts to a flanker. The bifocal series is a four-man backfield pattern run in an order of sequence. The quarterback reverse pivots and his first play is to hand the fullback who carries the ball through the 3 power hole. The second play is for

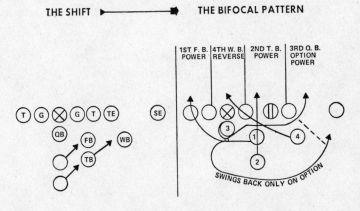

FIGURE 4-12: THE BIFOCAL SET

him to hand off to the tailback on a 2 power. The name bifocal was adopted because of the effect the fake of the fullback has on the defense. Actually, all the quarterback has to do is reverse pivot and the fullback will do the faking for him. On the third play he fakes to the tailback and options on a 6 power call. This is the only play in the sequence that the fullback swings back for the pitch out option after his fake. The fourth play is an inside reverse after a fake to the tailback. On this play the fullback's fake is an influence for the trapping tackle. This backfield sequence can be run to the left as well as to the right.

This concludes the complete framework of the system to put the multiple power "I" offense into application. A good philosophy for multiple application is to "Only use what you need, but if there is another need—you will have it." These multiple sets can be a big advantage to you if they are not misused. If they are not used correctly, you could hurt yourself. Never change the set when the offense is working for you. When you do change the set have a reason and a goal.

We have established that we use the same terms for coordination of our backfield techniques with our line blocking rules. From now on we will refer to them as plays. We will apply power plays, tandem plays and sweep plays to series and multiple application in the following six chapters.

CHAPTER 5

Applying Frontside Power Plays to Multiple Power "I" Series

Our power plays are an outgrowth of the Belly Split "T" offense. Today this same sequence has a different order of priorities and is thought of as something new: the triple option being run out of the wishbone formation. With the split "T" the quarterback keeper had priority over the pitchout in the option sequence. With the current wishbone the quarterback is trying to get the pitchout. Keeping the ball is second in priority on the option. In the triple option the quarterback has to key off of both the defensive tackle and defensive end.

Our fullhouse "I" backfield set is basically the same as the wishbone formation; our power play sequence is the same as the triple option sequence. The big difference is that we predetermine the hand-off to our fullback.

RELATING TO THE DIFFERENCES AND ADVANTAGES

We predetermine the hand-off to our fullback because of the multiple application of our power sequence. By doing this we cut our quarterback's decisions in half since he only has to option off of one defensive man. On an even series we can key all three plays of the power sequence off of the same defensive man. Applying our multiple system to these three plays takes the option far beyond its present approach. For us to run a true triple option with our fullback could result in breakdowns through our multiple application. Our power sequence has the same order of priorities as the triple option, even though we predetermine the fullback hand-off. It is to our advantage to prevent breakdowns and use multiple sets at the same time.

We have already discussed the very few breakdowns that have occurred along the way; now we need a solution for them. Let us review those problems and present their solutions:

1. Our one breakdown that occurred in our power blocking rules was against split 4 and 6 techniques (Figure 5-1). Our right guard was uncovered. His rules called for him to block the inside linebacker in front of him. The offensive tackle's rules called for him to block the defensive down lineman on his inside gap. Because of the defensive reach technique used on our offensive guard by their down lineman to the inside tackle gap, it made it impossible for our guard to carry out his assignment. *The solution* was for the guard to pull around his offensive tackle and seal at the point-of-attack (Figure 5-1).

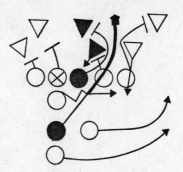

FIGURE 5-1

2. Our quarterback is under strict orders never to use 2 or 3 power calls in short yardage or goal line situations. The reason is because in these types of situations the defenses are usually set in all of the gaps of our inside holes (Figure 5-2). *The solution* is to substitute a 34 isolation play for the 32 power play (Figure 5-3). This has been our most consistent and dependable play.

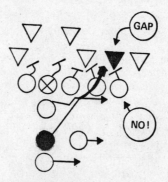

FIGURE 5-2

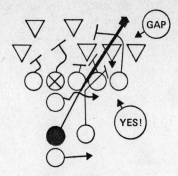

FIGURE 5-3

Another big difference in our power blocking rules has been that of our tight end. If no one is to his inside gap he will always block the first man off the line of scrimmage. On a 6 or 7 call he pulls and seals the first defensive man in pursuit (Figure 5-4). This has two unique advantages: it puts an extra man out in front of the pitch-out option, and it influences the defensive end to box and hesitate. The box will give the quarterback running room on the keeper back to the inside (Figure 5-5).

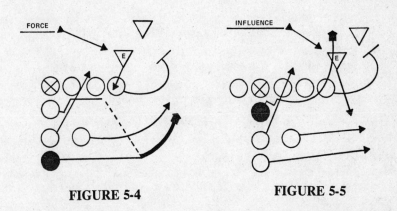

FIGURE 5-4   **FIGURE 5-5**

I want to reemphasize that the pitch-out is a high risk play and should never be called until it is well set up. In setting it up we use a combination of fullback powers with tandems and isolations. A few years ago we had a back score four long touchdowns in one game for a school record. He had only carried the ball seven times. We set it up with the split end set from the odd series call. When we made a 6 or 7 power call we set the split end to the call for the mirror block (Figure 5-6). Notice the blocking we had in front of him. The extra blocker is an additional feature that the wishbone does not use. These blockers also serve as an influence for the defense to overpursuit and leave the quarterback daylight to cut back toward midfield after a keeper.

We will next take a look at putting the power techniques and sequence into

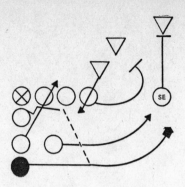

FIGURE 5-6

multiple application. We will show how we run the same power plays out of many formations against a variety of defenses.

We will establish a four-step format for putting the three power play sequence into application. The first step will be to adjust our offensive set to the defense. Each step will be illustrated by a figure as follows:

1. *First step* is to establish the offensive set against the defense that will be used throughout the sequence.

2. *Second step* is to apply the fullback play (2 or 3 calls) which is the first in the sequence against the established defense.

3. *Third step* is to apply the pitch-out from the option (6 or 7 calls) which is the second in the sequence, and has first priority in the option.

4. *Fourth step* is to apply the keeper from the option (6 or 7 calls) when the defensive end has left the quarterback without the pitch-out.

USING BALANCED LINES WITH 30 AND 40 FRONTSIDE SERIES

These are the frontside power plays with a balanced line. They feature the tailback to carry the ball on the pitchout, with the wingback the lead blocker out of the backfield. This frontside set also increases the threat to the defense since it is the tandem and sweep side. On the first sequence of the 30 series we will vary the defense as a lead and feeler situation. All the following sequences in the power series will use the four-step format.

We open with the power sequence within the 30 series that sets the split end from the call against a variety of defenses. In Figure 5-7 we run against a split 44 defense. This is the situation that forces our right guard to pull around the right tackle and seal on a "32 power-split left" play. In Figure 5-8 we run the same play against a 52 monster defense. Here the fullback cuts back into the pursuit after finding daylight. The quarterback has been keying on the defensive end during the past two plays. As a result it has been determined that the "36 power-split left" play has been set up (Figure 5-9). Though we run into a pro 43 defense our only concerns are the play of their defensive end and the positions of their fifth men. We get the pitch-out to the tailback behind the lead block of the wingback and the seal block of the tight end. Against a stack 44 the defensive end

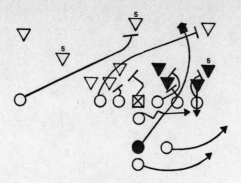

FIGURE 5-7: VS. SPLIT 44

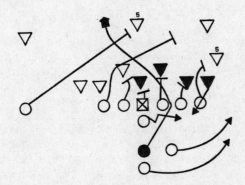

FIGURE 5-8: VS. 52 MONSTER

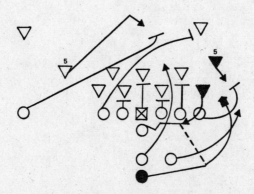

FIGURE 5-9: VS. PRO 43

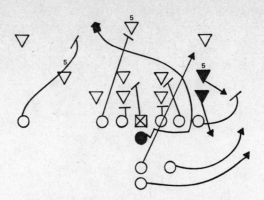

FIGURE 5-10: VS. STACK 44

is influenced by our pulling tight end and forces the quarterback to keep (Figure 5-10).

This sequence has offered about every situation we could possibly run into except an eight-man gap defense. We have never run into this much defense in our opening series. By the time we have run four plays we have usually been able to decide on the plays and formation we want to use.

The 52 monster defense is very popular today to use agianst the triple option. It is an outgrowth of the Oklahoma 54. The big difference is that it remains three deep. The monster usually plays to the side of our offensive set that is considered our strong side. We have seen some monsters that simply play the wide side of the field. If it is played this way we simply set our formation strong to the short side of the field and run in that direction. We consider the monster and safety as fifth men (Figure 5-11). The defensive end to split side is in a walkaway position.

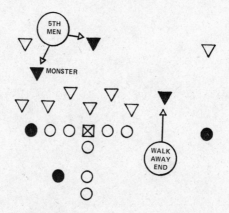

FIGURE 5-11: VS. 52 MONSTER

We will establish the set from which to run our 33-37 power sequence (Figure 5-11). The monster is playing our wingback side. Our wingback is set to the tight end's side. We set our split end from the call. This gives us our tandem side on their strongside and leaves us with a good backside attack.

Before we put the 33-37 power sequence into application we will establish the following blocking assignments that will be used against the 52 monster:

1. *Tight end*—(33 power play)—Near inside linebacker.
   (37 power play)—Pull left and seal.

2. *Left tackle*—On.

3. *Left guard*—Near linebacker.

4. *Center*—On.

5. *Right guard*—Near linebacker.

6. *Right tackle*—Check and release to Able.

7. *Split end*—Release to Baker (split right).

Next we will apply all three phases of this frontside running play sequence to the tight side:

1. *First phase* (Figure 5-12). In the 33 power play our fullback takes the hand-off over our uncovered left guard. He is forced to cut back because of the block on the linebacker. Their defensive end is closing down on our quarterback.

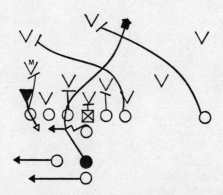

FIGURE 5-12: 33 POWER-SPLIT RIGHT

2. *Second phase* (Figure 5-13). On this 37 power play the monster is going for the fullback fake, and the defensive end forces the pitch-out. The tailback takes the pitch behind the leads of the wingback and tight end who are in good blocking positions.

3. *Third phase* (Figure 5-14). On this 37 power our tight end has influenced their defensive end to box forcing the quarterback to keep. He pitches after he clears the line of scrimmage.

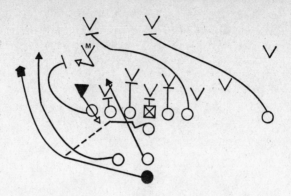

FIGURE 5-13: 37 POWER-SPLIT RIGHT

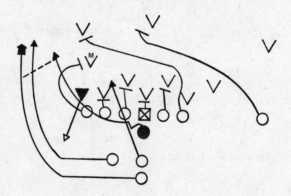

FIGURE 5-14: 37 POWER-SPLIT RIGHT

The 44 stack defense is a very popular stunting defense today. Any time our split end is double covered we feel that we have isolated two defensive men with one (Figure 5-15). Our split end fights to the outside to get down on his mirror block. This keeps the bump and run defensive man occupied with his vision from the play, and freezes the defensive half. We call even series plays with the split end to the call in these situations.

We will establish the set to run our 42-46 power sequence (Figure 5-15), set our split end to the even series call and run to the inside of the two isolated defensive men.

Before we put the 42-46 power sequence into application we will establish the following blocking assignments that will be used against the 44 stack:

1. *Right tackle*—On even series trade duties with tight end.
   (42 power play)—Near inside linebacker.
   (46 power play)—Pull right and seal.

2. *Right guard*—On.

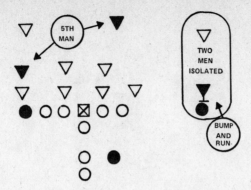

FIGURE 5-15: VS. 44 STACK

3. *Center*—Near outside linebacker.
4. *Left guard*—On.
5. *Left tackle*—Check and release to Charlie.
6. *Tight end*—Release to Baker.
7. *Split end*—Outside release for mirror block.

Next we will apply all three phases of this frontside running play sequence to the split side:

1. *First phase* (Figure 5-16)—On a 42 power our fullback takes the hand-off over right guard. This is the same as the triple option except that the quarterback has only one man off of which to option.

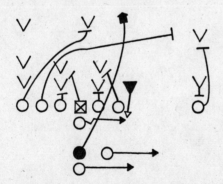

FIGURE 5-16: 42 POWER-SPLIT RIGHT

2. *Second phase* (Figure 5-17)—On this 46 power the defensive end forces the pitch-out.

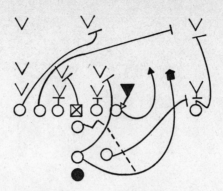

FIGURE 5-17: 46 POWER-SPLIT RIGHT

3. *Third phase* (Figure 5-18)—On this 46 power the defensive end is influenced to box by our pulling offensive tackle forcing the quarterback to keep.

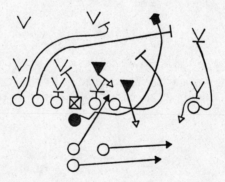

FIGURE 5-18: 46 POWER-SPLIT RIGHT

The pro 43 defense usually has prerotated inside, invert coverage. Sometimes the rotation takes place after the snap. The fifth men are the inverts (Figure 5-19). Against inverts the ball carriers should always be alert to cut back head on into the defensive rotation. This is because inverts have a natural tendency to overpursue. Because of this tendency we can use even series and set the split end to the call. We treat inverts in the same manner as we do the bump and run with double coverage.

We will establish the set to run our 43-47 power sequence (Figure 5-19). We will set our split end to the even series call.

Before we put 43-47 power sequence into application we will establish the following blocking assignments that will be used against the pro 43 defense:

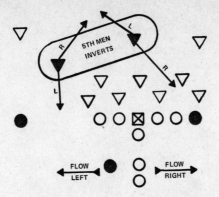

FIGURE 5-19: VS. 43 PRO INVERT

1. *Left tackle*—On even series trade duties with tight end.
   (43 power play)—Near linebacker.
   (47 power play)—Pull left and seal.
2. *Left guard*—On.
3. *Center*—Near linebacker.
4. *Right guard*—On.
5. *Right tackle*—Check and release to Able.
6. *Tight end*—Release to Baker.
7. *Split end*—Mirror block (split left).

Next we will apply all three phases of this frontside running play sequence to the split side:

1. *First phase* (Figure 5-20)—On 43 power our fullback takes the hand-off over left guard. The quarterback only has to key off the defensive end.

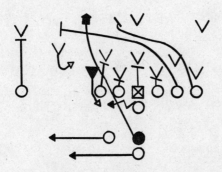

FIGURE 5-20: 43 POWER-SPLIT LEFT

2. *Second phase* (Figure 5-21)—On this 47 power the defensive end has forced our quarterback to pitch fast.

3. *Third phase* (Figure 5-22)—On this 47 power the inside defensive linebacker takes the fullback and the defensive end the tailback. This forces the quarterback to keep and pitch after he has cleared the line of scrimmage.

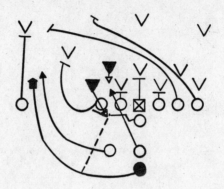

FIGURE 5-21: 47 POWER-SPLIT LEFT

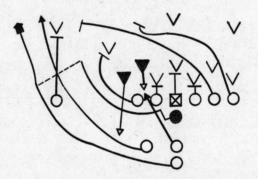

FIGURE 5-22: 47 POWER-SPLIT LEFT

USING UNBALANCED LINES WITH FRONTSIDE SERIES

We use the same frontside power plays with an unbalanced line. This again requires the tailback to carry the ball on a pitch out, with the wingback the lead blocker out of the backfield. The big difference is that we use the unbalanced lines to attack overshifting and undershifting defenses. We run to the strongside of an unbalanced line against the undershifted defenses, and run to the short side of the unbalanced line against the overshifted defenses.

When a defensive line completely shifts down with our unbalanced line, we then consider it an overshifted front. We can then attack the backside because we have a shorter distance to go in relation to their sets.

When the defense only has one fifth defensive man to our strongside and makes no line adjustment, we consider this an undershifted defense. We have run into this situation many times. We simply set our backfield to the strongside of an unbalanced line and run to that side.

On the 30 frontside series we set the split end to the call to get unbalanced lines. Most of the time 6-man lines that do not shift down are limited to adjustments on our strongside. A large percentage of them remain undershifted.

The split 6 defense (Figure 5-23) usually has a walkaway end to the shortside of our unbalanced line. On our strongside they have our gaps filled. They do not have the fifth man to our strongside. This makes it an undershifted defense. Because of the strongside gap situation we do not run the 2 power. We use a 4 isolation call in its place.

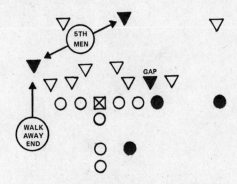

FIGURE 5-23: VS. SPLIT 6

We will establish the set to run our 34 isolation with our 36 power sequence (Figure 5-23). We will set our split end to the odd series call to get an unbalanced line to the right.

Before we put the 34 iso-36 power sequence into application we will establish the following blocking assignments that will be used against the split 6 defense:

1. *Tight end*—(34 iso)—Seal.
   (36 power)—Inside gap (has priority over pull and seal).
2. *Right tackle*—(34 iso)—Lead.
   (36 power)—Inside gap.
3. *Right guard*—(34 iso)—Post.
   (36 power)—Pull around tackle on split situation.
4. *Center*—Outside near linebacker.
5. *Left guard*—Outside gap.
6. *Left tackle*—Check and release to Charlie.
7. *Split end*—Mirror block (split right).

Next we will apply all three phases of this frontside running play sequence to tne strongside:

1. *First phase* (Figure 5-24). Because of the defensive gap situation at the point-of-attack we substitute 34 isolation in place of 32 power. Our most consistent short yardage plays have been 34 and 35 isolations.

2. *Second phase* (Figure 5-25). On this 36 power the defensive end has forced our quarterback to pitch. The tight end can not pull because of his inside gap priority.

3. *Third phase* (Figure 5-26). On this 36 power the defensive end boxes forcing our quarterback to keep.

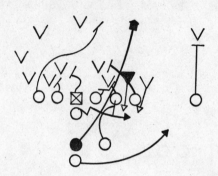

FIGURE 5-24: 34 ISO-SPLIT RIGHT

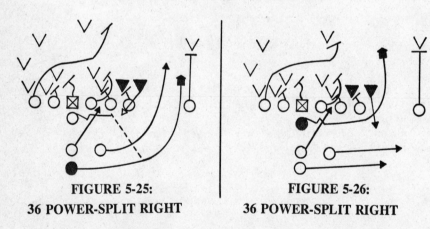

FIGURE 5-25:   **FIGURE 5-26:**

36 POWER-SPLIT RIGHT   **36 POWER-SPLIT RIGHT**

The wide tackle 6 defense (Figure 5-27) will also have a walkaway end to the shortside of our unbalanced line. Their shortside linebacker will usually double the guard. Their strongside tackle is in the defensive ends set and is not as well schooled in playing the option. Our quarterback will option off him. He will usually force the pitch. Again we have an undershifted defense.

We will establish the set to run our 33-37 power sequence (Figure 5-27), and set our split end to the odd series call to get an unbalanced line to the left.

Before we put our 33-37 power sequence into application we will establish the following blocking assignments that will be used against the wide tackle 6 defense:

1. *Tight end*—(33 power)—Near linebacker.
   (37 power)—Pull left and seal.
2. *Left tackle*—Near linebacker.
3. *Left guard*—On.
4. *Center*—Near outside linebacker.
5. *Right guard*—On.
6. *Right tackle*—Check and release to Able.
7. *Split end*—Mirror block (split left).

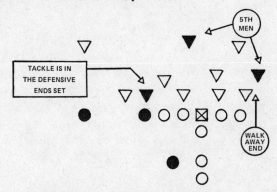

FIGURE 5-27: VS. WIDE TACKLE 6

Next we will apply all three phases of this frontside running play sequence to the strongside:

1. *First phase* (Figure 5-28). On a 33 power the fullback cuts back between the linebacker and center to set up the option.
2. *Second phase* (Figure 5-29). On this 37 power the defensive tackle forces our quarterback to pitch. When a defensive tackle is on our tight end we consider him the same as a defensive end.

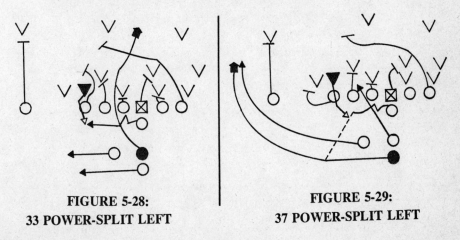

FIGURE 5-28:
33 POWER-SPLIT LEFT

FIGURE 5-29:
37 POWER-SPLIT LEFT

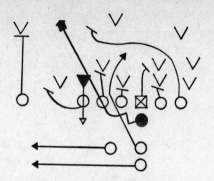

FIGURE 5-30: 37 POWER-SPLIT LEFT

3. *Third phase* (Figure 5-30). On this 37 power the pulling tight end has influenced the tackle wide forcing the quarterback to keep to his inside.

The overshifted 44 defense (Figure 5-31) is the most common defense to shift down one full man against our unbalanced line. The two fifth men are to our strongside. There are only 4 men to our shortside and they are in a position that gives us an angle advantage. We will attack the short side.

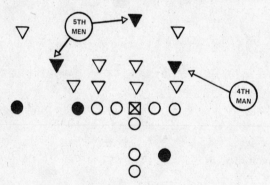

FIGURE 5-31: VS. OVERSHIFTED 44

We will establish the set to run 42-46 power sequence (Figure 5-31), and set our split end from the even series call in order to run to the shortside right of an unbalanced line.

Before we put our 42-46 power sequences into application we will establish the following blocking assignments that will be used against the overshifted 44 defense:

1. *Right tackle*—On even series trade duties with tight end.

(42 power)—Near linebacker.

(46 power)—Pull right and seal.

2. *Right guard*—Near inside linebacker.

3. *Center*—On.

4. *Left guard*—Near linebacker.

5. *Left tackle*—Check and release to Charlie.

6. *Tight end*—Release to Baker.

7. *Split end*—Release to Baker (split left).

Next we will apply all three phases of this frontside running play sequence to the shortside:

1. *First phase* (Figure 5-32). On this 42 power our fullback takes the hand-off. He is forced to cut back.

2. *Second phase* (Figure 5-33). On this 46 power the defensive end forces the pitch. This puts both our ball carrier and lead blockers around the corner in a hurry.

3. *Third phase* (Figure 5-34). On this 46 power the defensive end is influenced by our pulling tackle which forces our quarterback to keep.

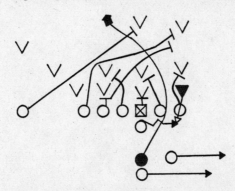

FIGURE 5-32: 42 POWER-SPLIT LEFT

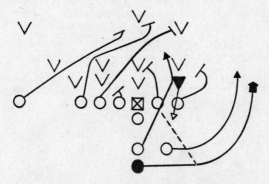

FIGURE 5-33: 46 POWER-SPLIT LEFT

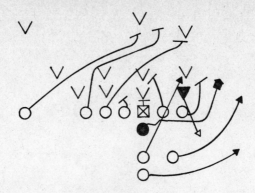

FIGURE 5-34: 46 POWER-SPLIT LEFT

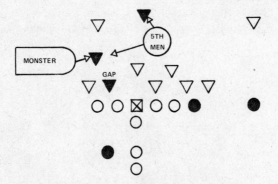

FIGURE 5-35: VS. OVERSHIFTED 52

The overshifted 52 defense (Figure 5-35) is not common but we have occasionally run into it. Most 52 defenses prefer to shift down only a half man, putting most of their down linemen in the gaps. We like to mix sweeps, reverses and tandems up the middle in with this sequence.

We will establish the set to run our 43-47 power sequence (Figure 5-35) and set our split end from the even series call in order to run shortside left of an unbalanced line.

Before we put our 43-47 power sequence into application we will establish the following blocking assignments that will be used against an overshifted 52 defense:

1. *Left tackle*—Inside gap priority.

2. *Left guard*—Near outside linebacker.

3. *Center*—Near linebacker.

4. *Right guard*—On.

5. *Right tackle*—Check and release to Able.

6. *Tight end*—Release to Baker.

7. *Split end*—Release to Baker (split right).

Next we will apply all three phases of this frontside running play sequence to the shortside:

1. *First phase* (Figure 5-36). On this 43 power there is a defensive tackle in the gap at the point-of-attack. After our fullback takes the hand-off he slides wide as he had predetermined before the snap.

2. *Second phase* (Figure 5-37). On this 47 power the defensive end has forced the quarterback to pitch fast. The ball carrier does not have far to go before turning the corner.

3. *Third phase* (Figure 5-38). On this 47 power the defensive end has forced the quarterback to keep and then pitches after he clears the line of scrimmage. A lot depends on their monster going for our fullback's fake.

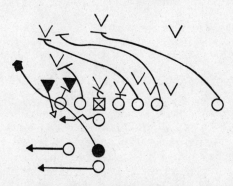

FIGURE 5-36: 43 POWER-SPLIT RIGHT

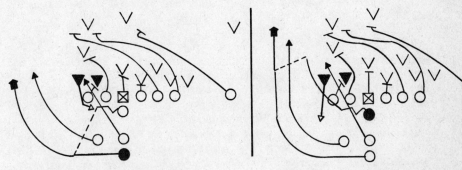

FIGURE 5-37: 47 POWER-SPLIT RIGHT

FIGURE 5-38: 47 POWER-SPLIT RIGHT

CHAPTER 6

Switching to Backside Power Plays

USING BALANCED LINE WITH 70 AND 80 BACKSIDE SERIES

Our power sequence has been more effective to the backside than to the frontside. There are three reasons for this. First, most defenses use one or two men to make a pre-snap set adjustment favoring our wingabck's side. Second, in selecting our personnel our wingback is usually a fast outside, open field type of runner, and our tailback is usually a power type of ball carrier. Third, on the 70 or 80 power sequence the wingback comes from the backside for the option pitch-out. The tailback is the lead blocker out of the backfield. The set is more suited to getting a proper pitchout relationship with the quarterback. On the 30 and 40 frontside power sequence it is a natural tendency for the tailback to get too far out in front of the quarterback to get a good pitch-out relationship. We have to work with this.

On our frontside series we have shown just about every kind of defensive concentration in relation to the variations of our multiple line sets. On the 70 and 80 backside series we will put more emphasis on the defensive concentration on our backfield sets and combine them with our multiple line sets. This will multiply the defensive situations so that we will have an advantage. By now you realize we have been running no more than the triple option sequence. Through our multiple sets we are able to take advantage of the defense which is not done in the current wishbone offense. This could easily be accomplished. In addition, we have yet to add our tandem and sweep plays that complement this power option sequence. On the 70 and 80 backside series we will show how we can take advantage of the fifth defensive men playing our wingback side.

The 53 eagle defense (Figure 6-1) presents two fifth men to the wingback side. It puts both down defensive tackles to the inside gap of our tackles. Here we

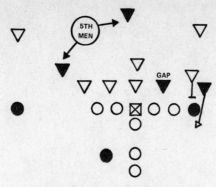

FIGURE 6-1: VS. 53 EAGLE

have a defensive linebacker that will use a bump and release technique on our tight end.

We will establish the set to run our 72-76 power sequence (Figure 6-1), set our split end from the odd series call to the wingback and run the plays to the tight end set away from the wingback.

Before we put our 72-76 power sequence into application we will establish the following blocking assignments to be used against the 53 eagle defense:

1. *Tight end*—(72 power play)—Near linebacker.
   (76 power play)—Pull right and seal.
2. *Right tackle*—Inside gap priority.
3. *Right guard*—Near linebacker.
4. *Center*—On.
5. *Left guard*—Outside gap.
6. *Left tackle*—Check and release to Charlie.
7. *Split end*—Release to Baker (split left).

Next we will apply all three phases of this backside running play sequence to the tight side:

1. *First phase* (Figure 6-2). On this 72 power there is a defensive tackle in the inside at the point-of-attack. After our fullback takes the hand-off he slides wide and then cuts back.
2. *Second phase* (Figure 6-3). On this 76 power the defensive end has forced the quarterback to pitch to the wingback behind the blocking of the tailback and tight end.
3. *Third phase* (Figure 6-4). On this 76 power the quarterback is forced to keep and slide wide.

The 52 monster defense (Figure 6-5) is playing their monster to our wingback side. Using the 70 or 80 backside power plays we can run away from him. Our backside plays should put us at a better advantage than our frontside attack.

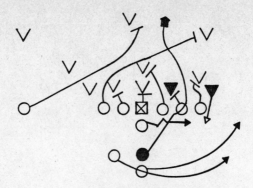

FIGURE 6-2: 72 POWER-SPLIT LEFT

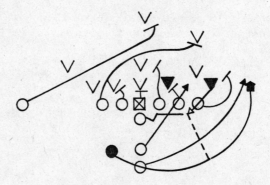

FIGURE 6-3: 76 POWER-SPLIT LEFT

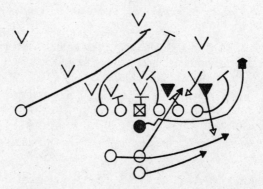

FIGURE 6-4: 76 POWER-SPLIT LEFT

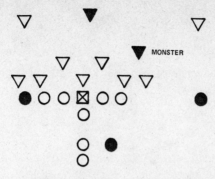

FIGURE 6-5: VS. 52 MONSTER

We will establish the set to run our 73-77 power sequence (Figure 6-5), set our split end from the wingback's side and run to the tight end's side of a balanced line.

Before we put our 73-77 power sequence into application we will establish the following blocking assignments that will be used against the 52 monster defense:

1. *Tight end*—(73 power)—Near linebacker is the halfback.
   (77 power)—Pull left and seal.

2. *Left tackle*—On.

3. *Left guard*—Near linebacker.

4. *Center*—On.

5. *Right guard*—Near linebacker.

6. *Right tackle*—Check and release to Able.

7. *Split end*—Release to Baker (split right).

Next we will apply all three phases of this backside running play sequence to the tight side:

1. *First phase* (Figure 6-6). On this 73 power the fullback takes the hand-off over left guard. Since there is no monster to that side the tight end blocks the halfback. The halfback can't come up as the monster could. This leaves a lot of running room.

2. *Second phase* (Figure 6-7). On this 77 power the defensive end forces the quarterback to pitch. This leaves the wingback with two blockers in front of him against the defensive halfback and pursuit.

3. *Third phase* (Figure 6-8). On this 77 power the defensive end forces the keeper. This is an ideal situation for the quarterback to pitch after he has cleared the line of scrimmage.

The 43 invert defense (Figure 6-9) has two inverts prerotated to our tandem side. They have to stop those plays. Using the 80 backside power series we can option all three plays of the sequence off the defensive end.

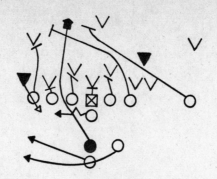

FIGURE 6-6: 73 POWER-SPLIT RIGHT

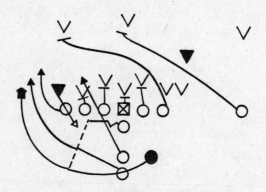

FIGURE 6-7: 77 POWER-SPLIT RIGHT

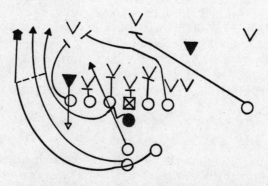

FIGURE 6-8: 77 POWER-SPLIT RIGHT

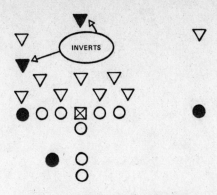

FIGURE 6-9: VS. 43 INVERT

We will establish the set to run our 82-86 power sequence (Figure 6-9), set our split end to the call for a mirror block and run all three plays off their defensive end.

Before we put our 82-86 power sequence into application we will establish the following blocking assignments that will be used against a 43 invert defense:

1. *Split end*—Mirror block—split right.
2. *Right tackle*—(82 power)—Near linebacker.
         (86 power)—Pull right and seal.
3. *Right guard*—On.
4. *Center*—Near linebacker.
5. *Left guard*—On.
6. *Left tackle*—Check and release to Charlie.
7. *Tight end*—Release to Baker.

Next we will apply all three phases of this backside running play sequence to the split side:

First phase (Figure 6-10). On this 82 power the fullback takes the hand-off. After running this play a couple of times the defensive end will begin to close down on the fullback.

Second phase (Figure 6-11). On this 86 power the quarterback is forced to pitch quick. The wingback does not have far to go to cut the corner with lots of blocking and open field in front of him.

Third phase (Figure 6-12). On this 86 power the quarterback is forced to keep. The pursuit will then force him to look for the pitch after he clears the line of scrimmage.

The undershifted 52 rover defense (Figure 6-13) is unusual. The five down linemen shift down one full man to our tight end side. Their two inside linebackers shift to our halfback set. The rover doubles behind the linebacker that is set in front of our center. This is so they are always in a position to adjust to our deployment.

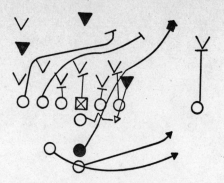

FIGURE 6-10: 82 POWER-SPLIT RIGHT

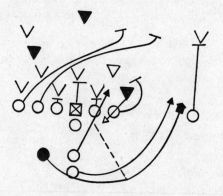

FIGURE 6-11: 86 POWER-SPLIT RIGHT

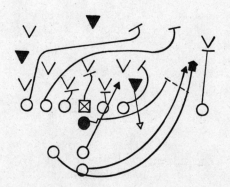

FIGURE 6-12: 86 POWER-SPLIT RIGHT

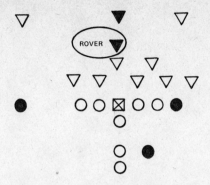

FIGURE 6-13: UNDERSHIFTED 52 ROVER

We will establish the set to run our 83-87 power sequence (Figure 6-13), set our split end to the call for a mirror block and run all three plays off their defensive end.

Before we put our 83-87 power sequence into application we will establish the following blocking assignment that will be used against a 52 rover defense:

1. *Split end*—Mirror block (split left).

2. *Left tackle*—(83 power)—Near linebacker.
   (87 power)—Pull left and seal.

3. *Left guard*—On.

4. *Center*—Near linebacker.

5. *Right guard*—On.

6. *Right tackle*—Check and release to Able.

7. *Tight end*—Release to Baker.

Next we will apply all three phases of this backside running play sequence to the split side:

First phase (Figure 6-14). On this 83 power the fullback takes the hand-off. Notice the quarterback has a natural key on the defensive end on all three plays.

Second phase (Figure 6-15). On this 87 power the quarterback has to pitch fast.

Third phase (Figure 6-16). On this 87 power the quarterback is forced to keep. After clearing the line of scrimmage do not pitch-out without a proper pitch-out relationship.

USING UNBALANCED LINES WITH THE BACKSIDE SERIES

The unbalanced lines can be incorporated into our backside attack in two ways. First if the defensive front refuses to adjust we can call the split end to the calls on the 70 series. Second, if the defense shifts down a half or full man to our strongside, we will set the split end from the calls on the 80 series. In addition, we still have the fifth defensive men making pre-snap adjustments to our front-

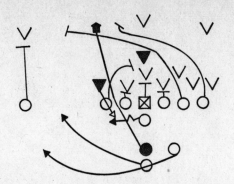

FIGURE 6-14: 83 POWER-SPLIT LEFT

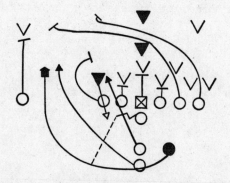

FIGURE 6-15: 87 POWER-SPLIT LEFT

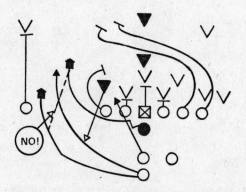

FIGURE 6-16: 87 POWER-SPLIT LEFT

side. This leaves us a lot of running room to our backside. By isolating their defensive half we have cleared out their defensive secondary to our backside before the ball is even snapped. All we have to do is break a ball carrier past the line of scrimmage to our backside.

In the remaining four power sequences we will first attack to the strongside of our unbalanced lines using the 70 backside series against undershifted defenses. Second we will attack the shortside of our unbalanced lines using the 80 backside series against defenses that have shifted down one half of a man. This would put defensive men in our gaps. In both cases we will show how the backside series will take advantage of prerotated invert and monsters who have set to our wingback's side. Our backside power sequences behind unbalanced lines have been more effective for us than they have been with balanced lines. Our backside power sequences have also been more effective than to the frontside. The reason we know this is that we have run many more power plays from our 70 and 80 series than we have from our 30 and 40 series.

The undershifted 52 defense (Figure 6-17) has their monster playing to the short side of our unbalanced line and to the frontside of our backfield set. Look at the open field past the line of scrimmage to our right side.

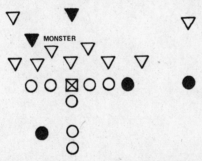

FIGURE 6-17: UNDERSHIFTED 52

We will establish the set to run our 72-76 power sequence (Figure 6-17) and set our split end to the call to get an unbalanced line strong right to the backside.

Before we put our 72-76 power sequence into application we will establish the following blocking assignments that will be used against an undershifted 52 defense:

1. *Split end*—Mirror block (split right).
2. *Tight end*—(72 power)—Near linebacker.
      (76 power)—Pull right and seal.
3. *Right tackle*—On.
4. *Right guard*—Near linebacker.
5. *Center*—On.
6. *Left guard*—Near linebacker.
7. *Left tackle*—Check and release to Charlie.

Next we will apply all three phases of this backside running play sequence to the strongside:

1. *First phase* (Figure 6-18). On this 72 power our fullback takes the hand-off over right guard and has plenty of running room once he is past the line of scrimmage.

2. *Second phase* (Figure 6-19). On this 76 power the quarterback is forced to pitch to the wingback who has two blockers and plenty of open field in front of him.

3. *Third phase* (Figure 6-20). On this 76 power the quarterback is forced to keep, and once past the line of scrimmage he has lots of daylight.

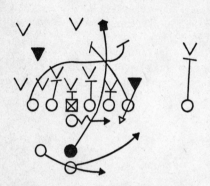

FIGURE 6-18: 72 POWER-SPLIT RIGHT

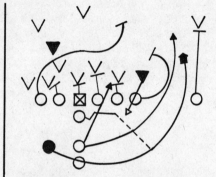

FIGURE 6-19: 76 POWER-SPLIT RIGHT

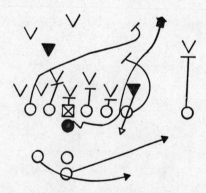

FIGURE 6-20: 76 POWER-SPLIT RIGHT

The undershifted 43 defense (Figure 6-21) has its two inverts prerotated to the shortside of our unbalanced line and to the frontside of our backfield set. Again we will have much open field to our left side once we are past the line of scrimmage.

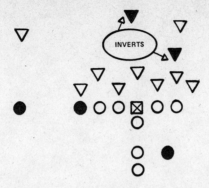

FIGURE 6-21: UNDERSHIFTED 43 INVERT

We will establish the set to run our 73-77 power sequence (Figure 6-21) and set our split end to the call to get an unbalanced line strong left to the backside.

Before we put our 73-77 power sequence into application we will establish the following blocking assignments that will be used against an undershifted 43 defense:

1. *Split end*—Mirror block (split left).
2. *Tight end*—(73 power)—Near linebacker.
                 (77 power)—Pull left and seal.
3. *Left tackle*—Near linebacker.
4. *Left guard*—On.
5. *Center*—Near linebacker.
6. *Right guard*—On.
7. *Right tackle*—Check and release to Able.

Next we will apply all three phases of this backside running play sequence to the strongside:

1. *First phase* (Figure 6-22). On this 73 power our fullback takes the hand-off through the left uncovered hole. In this case he is forced to slide to the outside because of the left tackle's block on the linebacker.
2. *Second phase* (Figure 6-23). On this 77 power the quarterback is forced to pitch to the wingback who has two blockers in front of him with plenty of open field.
3. *Third phase* (Figure 6-24). On this 77 power the quarterback is forced to keep and after he has cleared the line of scrimmage he discovers he has a good pitch-out relation with his wingback.

The gap 52 defense (Figure 6-25) is the result of the defensive front shifting down one half of a man. The monster is set to the strongside of an unbalanced line and to the frontside of our backfield set. There is a defensive lineman to the inside gap of our point-of-attack.

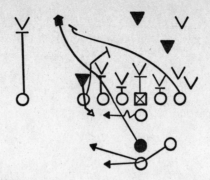

FIGURE 6-22: 73 POWER-SPLIT LEFT

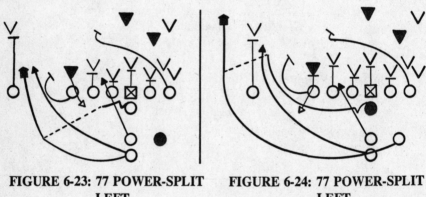

FIGURE 6-23: 77 POWER-SPLIT LEFT

FIGURE 6-24: 77 POWER-SPLIT LEFT

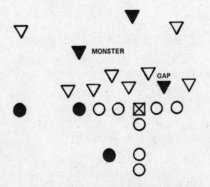

FIGURE 6-25: GAP SHIFT 52

We will establish the set to run our 82-86 power sequence (Figure 6-25) and set our split end from the call to get an unbalanced line shortside right. This will place the frontside of our backfield to the strongside of the unbalanced line for a backside attack.

Before we put our 82-86 power sequence into application we will establish the following blocking assignments against a gap 52 monster defense:

1. *Right tackle*—Inside gap.
2. *Right guard*—Near linebacker.
3. *Center*—Outside gap.
4. *Left guard*—Near linebacker.
5. *Left tackle*—Check and release to Charlie.
6. *Tight end*—Check and release to Baker.
7. *Split end*—Release to Baker.

Next we will apply all three phases of this backside running play sequence to the shortside:

1. *First phase* (Figure 6-26). On this 82 power our fullback takes the ball and slides to the outside of the right tackle gap as predetermined before the snap. All three plays in the sequence are keyed-off the defensive end.
2. *Second phase* (Figure 6-27). On this 86 power the quarterback pitches to the wingback who tries to turn the corner.
3. *Third phase* (Figure 6-28). On this 86 power the quarterback is forced to keep and as often happens, the pursuit forces him wide, leaving a poor pitch-out relationship.

The gap 43 defense (Figure 6-29) is the result of the defensive front shifting down one half of a man. The two inverts are prerotated to the strongside of an unbalanced line and to the frontside of our backfield set. Unlike the gap 52 defense there is no defensive lineman to our inside gap at the point-of-attack.

We will establish the set to run our 83-87 power sequence (Figure 6-29) and we will set our split end from the call to get an unbalanced line shortside left. This will set the frontside of our backfield to the strongside of the unbalanced line for a backside attack.

Before we put our 83-87 power sequence into application we will establish the following blocking assignments against a gap 43 invert defense:

1. *Left tackle*—(83 power)—Inside near linebacker.
              (87 power)—Pull left and seal.
2. *Left guard*—Inside gap.
3. *Center*—Near linebacker.
4. *Right guard*—Outside gap.
5. *Right tackle*—Check and release to Able.
6. *Tight end*—Release to Able.
7. *Split end*—Release to Baker.

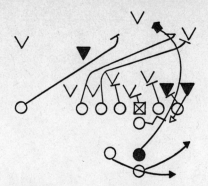

FIGURE 6-26: 82 POWER SPLIT LEFT

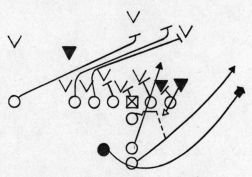

FIGURE 6-27: 86 POWER-SPLIT LEFT

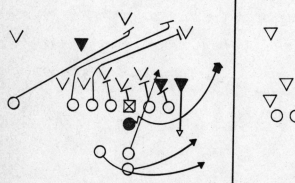

**FIGURE 6-28: 86 POWER-SPLIT
LEFT**

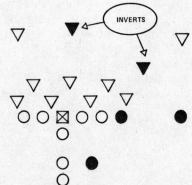

FIGURE 6-29: GAP SHIFT 43

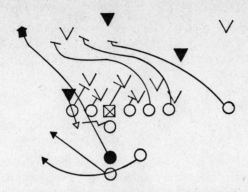

FIGURE 6-30: 83 POWER-SPLIT RIGHT

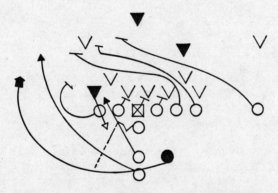

FIGURE 6-31: 87 POWER-SPLIT RIGHT

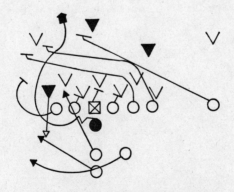

FIGURE 6-32: 87 POWER-SPLIT RIGHT

Next we will apply all three phases of this backside running play sequence:

1. *First phase* (Figure 6-30). On this 83 power our fullback takes the ball over our uncovered left guard. This leaves a big hole because of blocking angles; all three plays in the sequence can be keyed off the defensive end.

2. *Second phase* (Figure 6-31). On this 87 power the quarterback pitches to the wingback who turns the corner.

3. *Third phase* (Figure 6-32). On this 87 power the quarterback is forced to keep and then cut back against the pursuit.

This completes the multiple application of our power option sequence. You may find it hard to realize there have been only three basic running plays used through out these two chapters. Running the sequence to both sides makes a total of six basic running plays. We have run this sequence out of 16 formations, running 48 plays after learning to do only three things. Every time we changed a set we changed the situation: as we progressed we improved our advantage.

Now you should be able to see the two reasons why we were forced to predetermine the fullback and could not run a true triple option with our multiple sets. First, on even series either the defensive tackle or the end is often eliminated, leaving only one man from whom to key our option. This works to our advantage. Second, when we are running both to the strongside and shortside of unbalanced lines it kept it simple for our quarterback. To run a true triple option could cause breakdowns. We run the same sequence with equal effect, and our multiple sets have increased our advantages sixteenfold.

The power option sequence requires a lot of work and time to perfect. The quarterback has to learn to make a decision on the option, and to develop the timing with the rest of the backs to get a proper pitch out relationship. Even after the backfield timing is perfected, it still must be considered a high risk play. More practice time is required for work on the power option than on both our tandem and sweep plays put together. These plays will be covered in the following four chapters.

CHAPTER 7

How to Apply Tandem Plays to Multiple Power "I" Series

Our tandem plays are an outgrowth of the single wing offense. It is a fullhouse ''I'' backfield set behind single-wing blocking, featuring the tailback carrying the ball to the inside of the fullback and wingback using the tandem blocks on the first defensive down lineman to the outside of the hole. This is the 50 and 60 series call. Although our tandems are primarily for the tailback we do have a backside tandem where the wingback carries the ball from his halfback set. It is the same as a Missouri sweep action and uses a 70 series call. We also run fullback isolations. The frontside fullback isolations are run from the 30 series and the backside fullback isolations are run from the 90 series.

TANDEM SYNONYM AND THE ISO RELATIONSHIP

We have already established that isolation blocking is a half breed between power and tandem blocking rules. We use the tandem rules from the post man through the frontside and power rules from the post man through the backside. This means that no one pulls through the hole on an isolation call. On all isolation calls the wingback, from his halfback set, goes directly to the outside heel of the postman and blocks the first defensive man to show to the outside. The fullback leads through the hole and seals on 50 isolation calls, and carries the ball on 30 and 90 isolation calls. With an exception of 60 and 61 tandems, we always use odd series with tandem and isolation calls because we need the tight end set to the call to block off the line of scrimmage. Remember that all blockers and ball carriers run directly to the outside heel of the post man on all tandem and isolation techniques.

Before we put these plays into multiple application we need to establish a three-step format for better understanding:

1. *First step*—Establish the defense and manner in which blocking rules will be applied with both plays.

2. *Second step*—Show the isolation play.

3. *Third step*—Show the tandem play.

This will call for the use of three diagrams within the framework of one figure for illustrations.

USING THE 30, 50 AND 60 FRONTSIDE SERIES

54 isolation and tandem plays (Figure 7-1a) are shown against a 52 monster. Their monster is playing to our tight frontside to our right. They have a walkaway end to our split backside. Before we put 54 iso and tandem plays into application we will establish the following blocking assignments that will be used against the 52 monster defense:

1. *Tight end*—Near linebacker (monster).

2. *Right tackle*—Lead block (4 call man).

3. *Right guard*—Post block.

4. *Center*—On (power rule).

5. *Left guard*—54 iso—Near linebacker (power rule).
   54 tandem—Pull right through hole and seal.

6. *Left tackle*—54 iso—Check and release to Charlie.
   54 tandem—Cut-off.

7. *Split end*—Release to Baker (split left).

Next we will show these two frontside running plays to the right with the split end set from the call to get a balanced line:

1. *54 iso–split left* (Figure 7-1b). Our wingback goes to the outside heel of his right guard from his right half set. He blocks their defensive tackle out. The tailback takes the hand-off and follows the fullback through the 4 hole.

2. *54 tandem–split left* (Figure 7-1c). Our fullback and wingback tandem block the defensive tackle to the right. The tailback takes the hand-off and follows the pulling left guard through the 4 hole.

We will next run the same play to the other side against a different defensive situation.

55 isolation and tandem plays (Figure 7-2a) are shown against a 44 stack defense. The only adjustment that is made is their cornerback triangles our split side. The place to attack is to our tight side. Before we put 55 iso and tandem plays into application we will establish the following blocking assignments that will be used against the 44 stack defense:

1. *Tight end*—Near inside linebacker (seal).

2. *Left tackle*—Lead block (5 call man).

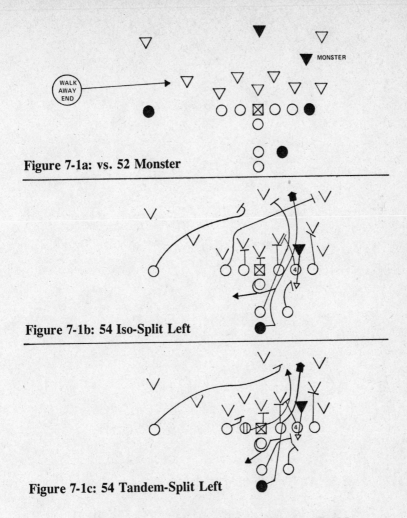

Figure 7-1a: vs. 52 Monster

Figure 7-1b: 54 Iso-Split Left

Figure 7-1c: 54 Tandem-Split Left

FIGURE 7-1: 54 ISOLATION AND TANDEM

3. *Left guard*—Post block.

4. *Center*—Near linebacker (power rule).

5. *Right guard*—55 iso—On (power rule).
   55 tandem—Pull left through hole and seal.

6. *Right tackle*—55 iso—Check and release to Able.
   55 tandem—Cut off.

7. *Split end*—Release to Baker (split right).

Next we will show these two frontside running plays to the left with the split end set from the call to get a balanced line:

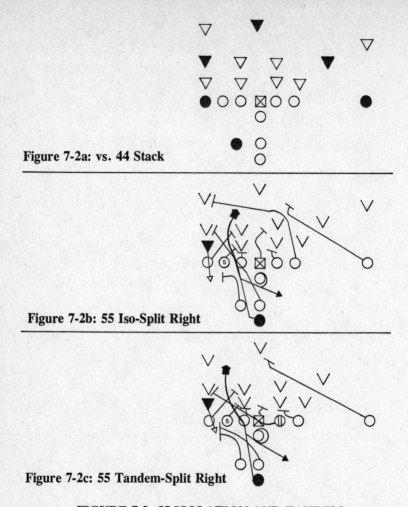

Figure 7-2a: vs. 44 Stack

Figure 7-2b: 55 Iso-Split Right

Figure 7-2c: 55 Tandem-Split Right

FIGURE 7-2: 55 ISOLATION AND TANDEM

1. *55 iso–split right* (Figure 7-2b). Our wingback goes to the outside heel of his left guard from his left half set and blocks their left tackle out. The tailback takes the hand-off and follows the fullback through the 5 hole.
2. *55 tandem–split right* (Figure 7-2c). Our fullback and wingback tandem the defensive left tackle. The tailback takes the hand-off and follows the pulling right guard through the 5 hole.

Next we will move the same plays one hole to the outside against two different defensive situations. It will make the tight end the call man and the tackles the post men. The outside heels of the tackles will be where the blocking and running backs will go to directly after the snap. The tailback will take the

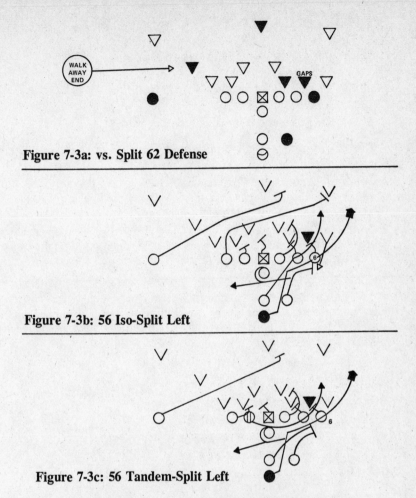

Figure 7-3a: vs. Split 62 Defense

Figure 7-3b: 56 Iso-Split Left

Figure 7-3c: 56 Tandem-Split Left

FIGURE 7-3: 56 ISOLATION AND TANDEM

same jab step, and the hand-off takes place in almost the same place as he did on the 4 and 5 holes. After he takes the hand-off he will need to slide wide.

56 isolation and tandem plays (Figure 7-3a) are shown against a split 62 defense. This presents two exceptional situations. The first is a defensive down lineman to the inside gap of the post man which eliminates the double team block to the inside of the 6 hole. Second, the right guard must pull around the tackle to block his linebacker because of the defensive tackle's reach technique. Before we put 56 iso and tandem plays into application we will establish the following blocking assignments against the split 62 defense:

1. *Tight end*—Lead block (6 call man).

2. *Right tackle*—Inside gap priority over post block.

3. *Right guard*—Pull around tackle to block linebacker.

4. *Center*—Near linebacker (power rule).

5. *Left guard*—56 iso—Outside gap (power rule).
   56 tandem—Pull right through hole and seal.

6. *Left tackle*—56 iso—Check and release to Charlie.
   56 tandem—Cut off.

7. *Split end*—Release to Baker (split left).

Next we show these two frontside running plays to the right tight side with the split end set from the call to get a balanced line:

1. *56 iso–split left* (Figure 7-3b). Our wingback goes to the outside heel of his right tackle and blocks their end out. The tailback takes the hand-off and follows the fullback through the 6 hole.

2. *56 tandem–split left* (Figure 7-3c). Our fullback and wingback tandem the defensive right end. The tailback takes the hand-off and follows the pulling left guard through the 6 hole. This is predetermined.

57 isolation and tandem plays (Figure 7-4a) are shown against a 43 invert defense. The invert are prerotated to the strongside. In this situation the post and lead block will be on the outside linebacker. Before we put 57 iso and tandem plays into application we will establish the following blocking assignments against the 43 invert defense:

1. *Tight end*—Lead block (7 call).

2. *Left tackle*—Post block.

3. *Left guard*—On (power rule).

4. *Center*—Near linebacker (power rule).

5. *Right guard*—57 iso—On (power rule).
   57 tandem—Pull left through 7 hole.

6. *Right tackle*—57 iso—Check and release to Able.
   57 tandem—Cut-off.

7. *Split end*—Release to Baker (split right).

Next we show these two frontside running plays to the left side with the split end set from the call to get a balanced line:

1. *57 iso–split right* (Figure 7-4b). Our wingback goes to the outside heel of his left tackle and blocks their end out. The tailback takes the hand-off and follows fullback through the 7 hole.

2. *57 tandem–split right* (Figure 7-4c). Our fullback and wingback tandem the left end. The tailback takes the hand-off and follows the pulling right guard through the 7 hole.

We will next show how we split an even defense. We have been very effective with our 60 and 61 tandems by running them right up the middle.

60 and 61 tandem plays (Figure 7-5a) are shown against a 44 stack defense. Here we have their set to our right split side. In Figure 7-5c we will use this same

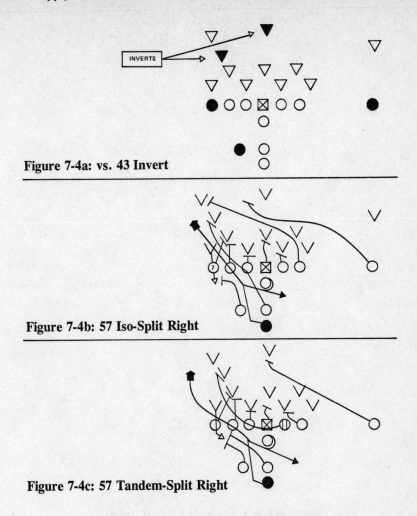

Figure 7-4a: vs. 43 Invert

Figure 7-4b: 57 Iso-Split Right

Figure 7-4c: 57 Tandem-Split Right

FIGURE 7-4: 57 ISOLATION AND TANDEM

defensive set adjustment to the left. Before we put 60 and 61 tandems into application we will establish the following blocking assignments against the 44 stack defense:

1. *Split side tackles*—Inside linebacker.
2. *Split side guards*—Seal block.
3. *Center*—Lead (call man).
4. *Tight side guards*—Post block.
5. *Tight side tackles*—Pull through the hole.

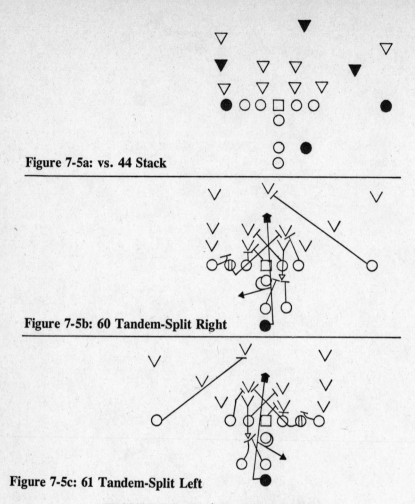

Figure 7-5a: vs. 44 Stack

Figure 7-5b: 60 Tandem-Split Right

Figure 7-5c: 61 Tandem-Split Left

FIGURE 7-5: 60 AND 61 TANDEMS

    6. *Tight end*—Cut-off.

    7. *Split end*—Release to Baker.

Next we show these two frontside running plays to the split side to get a balanced line:

    1. *60 tandem–split right* (Figure 7-5b). Our fullback and wingback tandem the first defensive lineman on the line of scrimmage to the right of center. The tailback takes the hand-off and follows the pulling left tackle up the middle.

    2. *61 tandem–split left* (Figure 7-5c). Our fullback and wingback tandem the first defensive lineman on the line of scrimmage to the left of center.

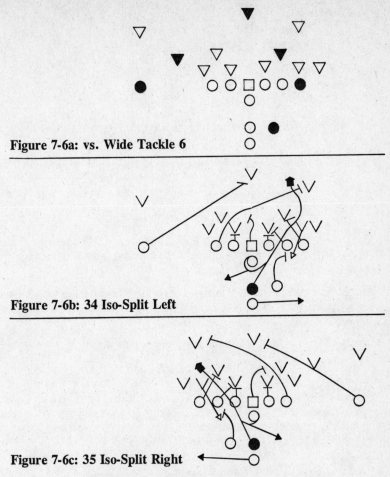

Figure 7-6a: vs. Wide Tackle 6

Figure 7-6b: 34 Iso-Split Left

Figure 7-6c: 35 Iso-Split Right

FIGURE 7-6: 34 AND 35 ISOLATIONS

The tailback takes the hand-off and follows the pulling right tackle up the middle.

Next we will show the fullback isolation plays. These are the plays with which we replace the fullback power plays in gap or short yardage situations. They have been our most consistent plays.

34 and 35 isolation plays (Figure 7-6a) are shown against a wide tackle 62 defense. Here we show the set to our right tight side. In Figure 7-6c we will use the same defensive set adjustment to the left. Before we put 34 and 35 isos into application we will establish the following blocking assignments against the wide tackle 62 defense:

1. *Tightside tight end*—Seal.

2. *Tightside tackles*—Lead (call man).

3. *Tightside guards*—Post.

4. *Center*—Near linebacker (power rule).

5. *Splitside guards*—On (power rule).

6. *Splitside tackles*—Check and release (power rule).

7. *Split end*—Release to Baker.

Next we show these two frontside running plays to the tight side of a balanced line:

1. *34 iso–split left* (Figure 7-6b). Our wingback goes to the outside heel of the right guard from his right half set and blocks their defensive tackle out. The fullback takes the hand-off from that same spot through the 4 hole.

2. *35 iso–split right* (Figure 7-6c). Our wingback goes to the outside heel of the left guard from his left half set and blocks their defensive tackle out. The fullback takes the hand-off from that same spot through the 5 hole.

This completes our frontside isolation and tandem plays behind a balanced line. We will next show them behind an unbalanced line which will create new and different defensive situations.

APPLYING UNBALANCED LINES TO FRONTSIDE PLAYS

To get unbalanced lines we call the split end to the call on 30 and 50 isolation plays, and from the call on 60 tandem plays. This will result in the 30 and 50 series being run to the strongside of an unbalanced line, and the 60 series being run to the shortside of an unbalanced line. Against our 30 and 50 series we will show the defense shifted down one half of a man. We will show this same shift against our 60 series, plus a monster set to our frontside. This will present us with a realistic situation and show that we have no problems adjusting to changing situations. Actually the defense is having to make the adjustments instead of the offense.

The 60 and 61 calls are the only tandem plays we run to the shortside of an unbalanced line. We could run other tandem or isolation plays without a tight end to the call, but we prefer to leave a weak tendency, rather than shortchanging ourselves one man. It has been our experience that we are more effective with our split end not taking near the split with tandem and isolation plays as he did with the power plays. This is because in power plays we were spreading and clearing out areas for the breakaways. With tandem plays we are bunching up on the defense. It has "five yards and a cloud of dust" characteristics. It is not designed to fool anyone. Defensive players have a tendency to get in their own player's way. This causes the unbalanced lines to take on more importance than they did in the power plays. The tandem plays are very punishing to the defense and do not require nearly as much time to perfect as did the power sequence.

Our split ends usually split 5 to 6 yards on the tandem and isolation plays instead of the usual 10 to 15 yards. This increases the pressure on the defensive front to the strongisde of our unbalanced lines. We do not worry about it putting

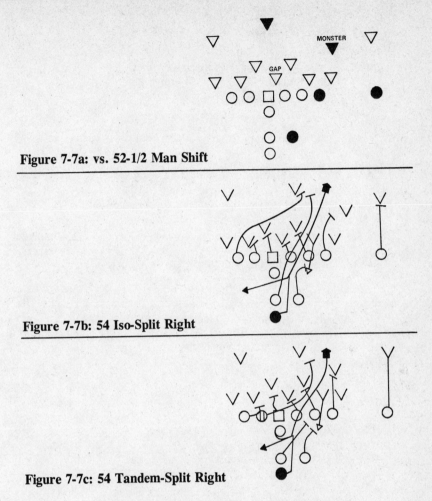

Figure 7-7a: vs. 52-1/2 Man Shift

Figure 7-7b: 54 Iso-Split Right

Figure 7-7c: 54 Tandem-Split Right

FIGURE 7-7: 54 ISOLATION AND TANDEM

less pressure on their defensive secondary because we are not trying for long yardage.

54 isolation and tandem plays (Figure 7-7a) are shown against a 52 monster defense shifted down one half of a man to the strongside of an unbalanced line. This puts a defensive down lineman in our post man's inside gap which will eliminate our double team block to the inside of the hole. Before we put 54 isolation and tandem into application we will establish the following blocking assignments against the 52 monster defense:

1. *Split end*—Mirror block (split right).
2. *Tight end*—Near linebacker (monster).

    3. *Right tackle*—Lead block on near inside linebacker (call man).

    4. *Right guard*—Inside gap priority over post block.

    5. *Center*—Near linebacker (power rule).

    6. *Left guard*—54 iso—Outside gap (power rule).
                   54 tandem—Pull right through hole.

    7. *Left tackle*—54 iso—Check and release to Charlie.
                   54 tandem—Cut off.

Next we will show these two frontside running plays to the strong side of an unbalanced line:

    1. 54 iso split right (Figure 7-7b). Our wingback goes to the outside heel of the right guard from his right half set and blocks their defensive tackle out. The tailback takes the hand-off and follows the fullback through the 4 hole.

    2. 54 tandem split right (Figure 7-7c). Our wingback and fullback tandem block the defensive tackle outside the 4 hole. The tailback takes the hand-off and follows his pulling left guard through the hole.

55 isolation and tandem plays (Figure 7-8a) are shown against a 44 stack defense shifted down one half of a man to the strong side of an unbalanced line. This sets the defensive down lineman to the inside gap of the lead man. Now we can get the double team block. Before we put 55 isolation and tandem into application we will establish the following blocking assignments against the 44 stack defense:

    1. *Split end*—Mirror block (split left).

    2. *Tight end*—Seal block.

    3. *Left tackle*—Lead block.

    4. *Left guard*—Post block.

    5. *Center*—Outside gap (power rule).

    6. *Right guard*—55 iso—Power rule.
                   55 tandem—Pull left through 5 hole.

    7. *Right tackle*—55 iso—Check and release to Able.
                   55 tandem—Cut-off.

Next we will show these two frontside running plays to the strong side of an unbalanced line:

    1. 55 iso–split left (Figure 7-8b). Our wingback goes to the outside heel of the left guard and blocks their defensive end out. The tailback takes the hand-off and follows the fullback through the 5 hole.

    2. 55 tandem–split left (Figure 7-8c). Our fullback and wingback tandem their defensive end outside the 5 hole. The tailback takes the hand-off and follows his pulling right guard through the 5 hole.

Next we will move these same plays out one hole. Any time you can get the defense to shift down one half of a man to the strongside of an unbalanced line,

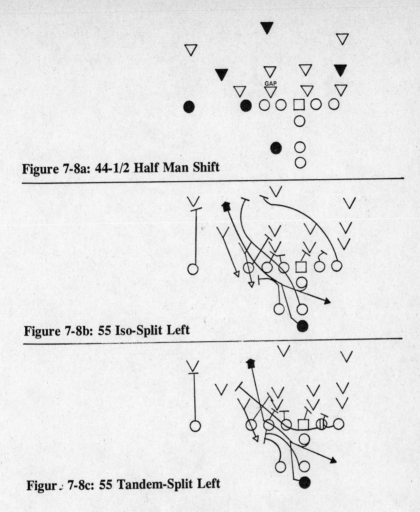

Figure 7-8a: 44-1/2 Half Man Shift

Figure 7-8b: 55 Iso-Split Left

Figur. 7-8c: 55 Tandem-Split Left

FIGURE 7-8: 55 ISOLATION AND TANDEM

and get them in our gaps, calling the 6 and 7 holes are to our advantage. This is because once we break the tailback past the line of scrimmage, he has a lot of running room to the outside.

In attacking the strongside of an unbalanced line the situation will determine if we run to the inside or outside holes. If they have a fifth man, such as a corner back, monster or invert, we will use the 4 and 5 holes and run to their inside. If there is no fifth man in the area we will run the 6 and 7 holes to the outside. Regardless of what your system is, you should have some play of this type that you can run at both these inside and outside holes depending on the situation. If a defensive end begins to punish your quarterback on the option, you need to be able to return the punishment with these types of plays. Any time we catch a

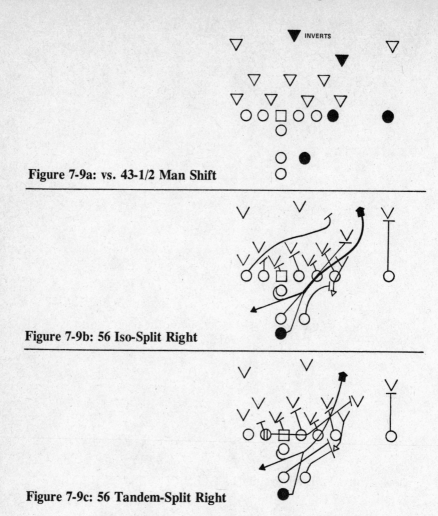

Figure 7-9a: vs. 43-1/2 Man Shift

Figure 7-9b: 56 Iso-Split Right

Figure 7-9c: 56 Tandem-Split Right

FIGURE 7-9: 56 ISOLATION AND TANDEMS

forcing end hitting our quarterback after he has handed off on a fullback power, we are going to run some 6 and 7 tandems at him. This is a very effective counter action.

56 isolation and tandem plays (Figure 7-9a) are shown against a 43 invert defense shifted down to our strongside one half of a man. This eliminates our double team block to the inside of the hole because there is a defensive down lineman to the inside gap of our post man. Before we put 56 isolation and tandem plays into application we will establish the following blocking assignments against the 43 invert defense:

1. *Split end*—Mirror block (split right).
2. *Tight end*—Lead block (6 call man).

3. *Right tackle*—Inside gap priority over post block.

4. *Right guard*—Near linebacker (power rule).

5. *Center*—Outside gap (power rule).

6. *Left guard*—56 iso—Power rule.
                56 tandem—Pull right through 6 hole.

7. *Left tackle*—56 iso—Check and release to Charlie.
                56 tandem—Cut off.

Next we will show these two frontside running plays to the strongside of an unbalanced line:

1. *56 iso–split right* (Figure 7-9b). Our wingback goes to the outside heel of the right tackle and blocks their defensive end out. The tailback takes the hand-off and follows the fullback through the 6 hole.

2. *56 tandem–split right* (Figure 7-9c). Our fullback and wingback tandem the defensive end outside the 6 hole. The tailback takes the hand-off and follows the pulling right guard through the 6 hole.

57 isolation and tandem plays (Figure 7-10a) are shown against a tight 62 defense shifted down to our strongside one half of a man. Again the double team block to the inside of the 7 hole is eliminated because there is a defensive down lineman to the inside gap of our post man. Before we put 57 isolation and tandem plays into application we will establish the following blocking assignment against the tight 62 defense:

1. *Split end*—Mirror block (split left).

2. *Tight end*—Lead block (7 call man).

3. *Left tackle*—Inside gap priority over post block.

4. *Left guard*—Near linebacker (power rule).

5. *Center*—Outside gap (power rule).

6. *Right guard*—57 iso—Power rule.
                57 tandem—Pull left through 7 hole.

7. *Right tackle*—57 iso—Check and release to Able.
                57 tandem—Cut off.

Next we will show these two frontside running plays to the strongside of an unbalanced line:

1. *57 iso–split left* (Figure 7-10b). Our wingback goes to the outside heel of the left tackle and blocks their defensive end out. The tailback takes the hand-off and follows the fullback through the hole.

2. *57 tandem–split left* (Figure 7-10c). Our fullback and wingback tandem the defensive end outside the 7 hole. The tailback takes the hand-off and follows the pulling left guard through the 7 hole.

Next we will run these frontside tandems to the shortside of an unbalanced line. We use the 60 series for the calls.

60 and 61 tandem plays (Figure 7-11a) are shown against a 52 monster defense shifted down to our strongside one half of a man. Before we put 60 and

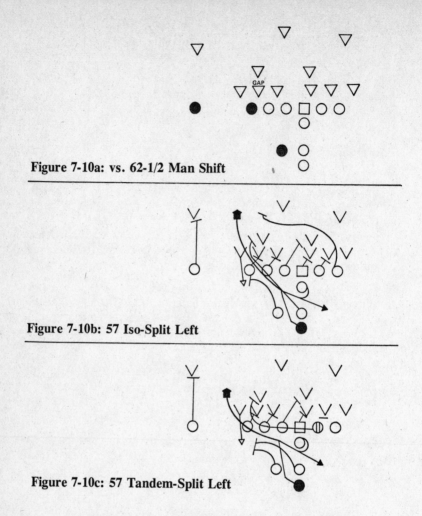

Figure 7-10a: vs. 62-1/2 Man Shift

Figure 7-10b: 57 Iso-Split Left

Figure 7-10c: 57 Tandem-Split Left

FIGURE 7-10: 57 ISOLATION AND TANDEM

61 tandems into application we will establish the following blocking assignments against the 52 monster defense:

1. *Shortside tackles*—Near linebacker (monster).
2. *Shortside guards*—Seal.
3. *Center*—Lead block (call man).
4. *Strongside guards*—Post block.
5. *Strongside tackles*—Pull through hole.
6. *Tight end*—Cut off.
7. *Split end*—Release to Baker.

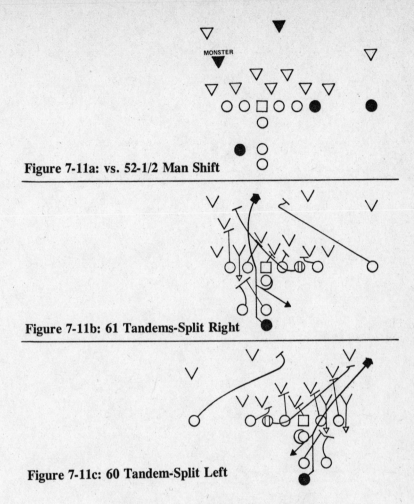

Figure 7-11a: vs. 52-1/2 Man Shift

Figure 7-11b: 61 Tandems-Split Right

Figure 7-11c: 60 Tandem-Split Left

FIGURE 7-11: 60 AND 61 TANDEMS

Next we will show these two frontside running plays to the shortside of an unbalanced line:

1. *61 tandem–split right* (Figure 7-11b). Our fullback and wingback tandem the first defensive lineman on the line of scrimmage to the left of center. The tailback takes the hand-off and follows the pulling right tackle through the 1 hole.

2. *60 tandem–split left* (Figure 7-11c). Our fullback and wingback tandem the first defensive lineman on the line of scrimmage to the right of center. The tailback takes the hand-off and follows the pulling left tackle through the 0 hole.

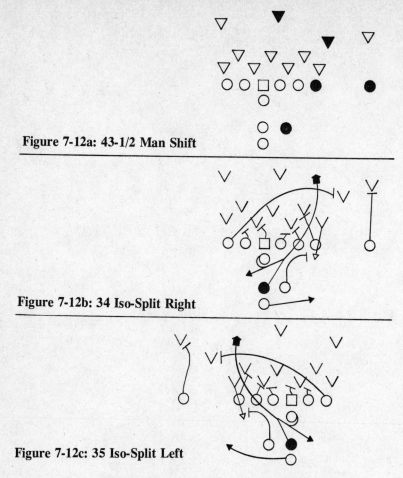

Figure 7-12a: 43-1/2 Man Shift

Figure 7-12b: 34 Iso-Split Right

Figure 7-12c: 35 Iso-Split Left

FIGURE 7-12: 34 AND 35 ISOLATIONS

34 and 35 isolation plays (Figure 7-12a) are shown against a 43 invert defense shifted down to our strongside one half of a man. This gives us a natural hole. Before we put 34 and 35 isos into application we will establish the following blocking assignments against the 43 invert defense:

1. *Split end*—Mirror block (set to the call).
2. *Tight end*—Seal block.
3. *Strongside tackles*—Lead block (call man).
4. *Strongside guards*—Post block.
5. *Center*—Outside gap (power rule).
6. *Shortside guards*—Near linebacker (power rule).
7. *Shortside tackles*—Check and release (power rule).

Next we show these two frontside running plays to the strongside of an unbalanced line:

1. *34 iso–split right* (Figure 7-12b). Our wingback goes to the outside heel of the right guard from his right half set and blocks their defensive tackle out.

2. *35 iso–split left* (Figure 7-12c). Our wingback goes to the outside heel of the left guard from his left half set and blocks the defensive tackle out.

This completes our frontside attack. Outside of the fullback isolations the tailback has carried the ball on all of our frontside plays. Our tailback does not carry the ball in the backside attack.

CHAPTER 8

Developing Backside Tandem Plays

The wingback carries the ball on 70 and 80 tandem series. He sets in his halfback position away from the call. On the snap the quarterback pivots to the wingback and pitches the ball to him before leading him through the hole. The fullback and tailback tandem the first defensive lineman to the outside of the hole. The backside guard pulls and leads the wingback through the hole along with the quarterback. There is the usual double team block to the inside of the hole. Like a single wing it develops slowly in order to get that many people to the point-of-attack. The timing is natural and very effective. This backfield action is better known as the Missouri Sweep Action.

The fullback carries the ball on 90 series isolation calls. These are the same plays as the 34 and 35 isolations except that they are run to the backside of a floater T backfield set. This is the first time up until now that we have shifted out of the fullhouse "I" backfield set. We need these plays in short yardage situations when we are often running from the 10 and 20 frontside series and 90 backside series. This is because the shifts and backfield sets are the same.

The 80 series tandems are run to the split side of a balanced line or the shortside of an unbalanced line. The timing is much better at the 6 and 7 holes than at the 4 or 5 holes. We do not have a tight end for a 6 or 7 call on the 80 series. Because of this we will only show the 70 tandems. If we needed to run a wingback tandem to the shortside of an unbalanced line we would simply call it out of the 80 series and set the split end from the call. As originally stated, we don't install anything we don't use; but if we need it—we have it.

To put the 70 and 90 backside series into application behind balanced lines we set the split end from the call. This sets the wingback to the split side; we run the plays to the tight side.

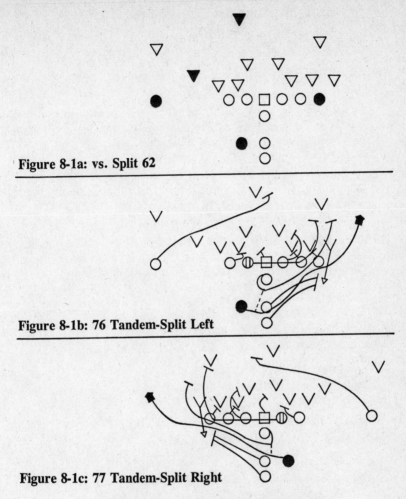

Figure 8-1a: vs. Split 62

Figure 8-1b: 76 Tandem-Split Left

Figure 8-1c: 77 Tandem-Split Right

FIGURE 8-1: 76 AND 77 TANDEMS

76 and 77 tandem plays (Figure 8-1a) are shown against a split 62 defense. This leaves gap situations to the tight side and eliminates our double team block to the inside of the holes:

Before we put 76 and 77 tandems into application we will establish the following blocking assignments against the split 62 defense:

1. *Tight end*—Lead block.
2. *Tightside tackles*—Inside gap priority over post block.
3. *Tightside guards*—Pull around tackle to block linebacker.
4. *Center*—Near linebacker (power rule).

5. *Splitside guards*—Pull and lead through the holes.

6. *Split side tackles*—Cut-off block.

7. *Split end*—Release to Baker (set from call).

Next we will show these two backside running plays to the tight side of a balanced line:

1. *76 tandem–split left* (Figure 8-1b). Our quarterback reverse pivots and pitches to the wingback before leading him through the 6 hole along with the pulling left guard. The fullback and tailback tandem the defensive end set to the outside of the 6 hole.

2. *77 tandem–split right* (Figure 8-1c). Our quarterback reverse pivots and pitches to the wingback before leading him through the 7 hole along with pulling right guard. The fullback and tailback tandem the defensive end set to the outside of the 7 hole.

To run the fullback isolations to our backside we have to use a 90 series shift. The wingback shifts to a flanker position from his halfback set away from the call. The tailback shifts to a halfback set to the call. If the fifth men are in the defense or favoring our flanker side we will have plenty of open field to the backside.

94 and 95 isolation plays (Figure 8-2a) are shown against a wide tackle 62 defense. Before we put these plays into application we will establish the following blocking assignments against the 62 defense:

1. *Tight end*—Seal block.

2. *Tight side tackles*—Lead block (call man).

3. *Tight side guards*—Post block.

4. *Center*—Near linebacker (power rules).

5. *Split side guards*—On (power rules).

6. *Splitside tackles*—Check and release (power rules).

7. *Split end*—Release to Baker (set from call).

Next we will show these two backside running plays run to the tight side of a balanced line:

1. *94 iso–split left* (Figure 8-2b). The tailback goes to the outside heel of the right guard and traps out. The fullback takes the hand-off through the 4 hole.

2. *95 iso–split right* (Figure 8-2c). The tailback goes to the outside heel of the left guard and traps out. The fullback takes the hand-off through the 5 hole.

Next we will run these same backside running plays behind an unbalanced line.

APPLYING UNBALANCED LINES TO BACKSIDE PLAYS

If the monsters or inverts set to our wingback side, and their defensive front does not shift down to the strongside of our unbalanced line, we use the backside

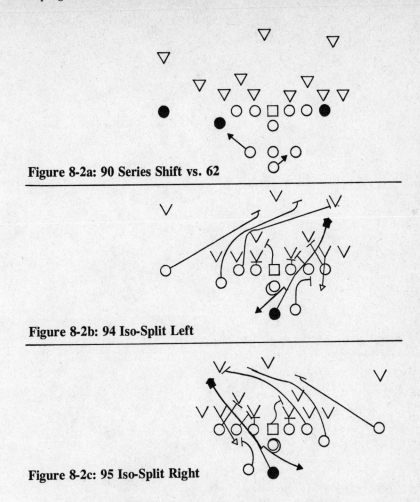

Figure 8-2a: 90 Series Shift vs. 62

Figure 8-2b: 94 Iso-Split Left

Figure 8-2c: 95 Iso-Split Right

FIGURE 8-2: 94 AND 95 ISOLATIONS

plays. We get an unbalanced line by setting the split end to the call on the 70 and 90 series calls. This will give us plenty of daylight to the strongside.

76 and 77 tandem plays (Figure 8-3a) are shown against a 43 invert defense. The fifth men are prerotated to the wingbacks' side, leaving a natural hole to the strongside of our unbalanced line. Before we put these plays into application we will establish the following blocking assignments against the 43 defense:

1. *Split end*—Mirror block (set to call).
2. *Tight end*—Lead block (call man).
3. *Strongside tackles*—Inside gap priority over post block.
4. *Strongside guards*—Inside linebacker (power rule).

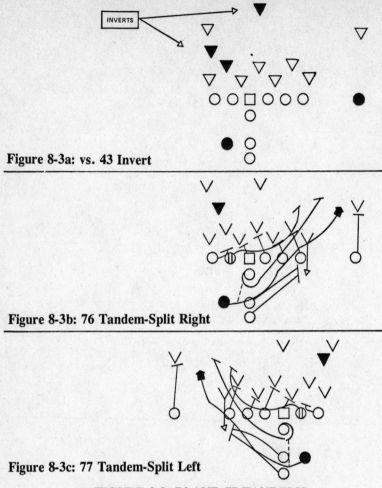

Figure 8-3a: vs. 43 Invert

Figure 8-3b: 76 Tandem-Split Right

Figure 8-3c: 77 Tandem-Split Left

FIGURE 8-3: 76 AND 77 TANDEMS

5. *Center*—Outside gap (power rule).

6. *Shortside guards*—Pull through holes called.

7. *Shortside tackles*—Cut off.

Next we will show these two backside running plays to the strongside of an unbalanced line:

1. *76 tandem–split right* (Figure 8-3b). We run our wingback tandem play to the strong right side of an unbalanced line.

2. *77 tandem–split left* (Figure 8-3c). We run our wingback tandem play to the strong left side of an unbalanced line.

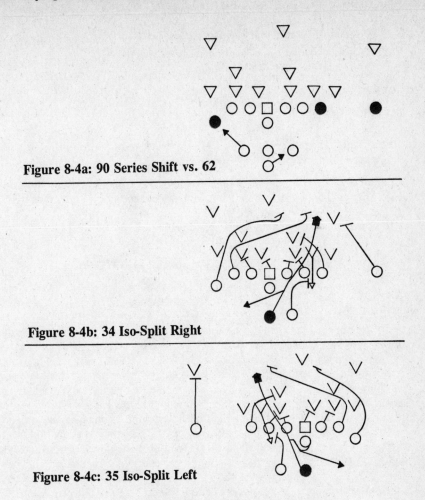

Figure 8-4a: 90 Series Shift vs. 62

Figure 8-4b: 34 Iso-Split Right

Figure 8-4c: 35 Iso-Split Left

FIGURE 8-4: 94 AND 95 ISOLATIONS

94 and 95 isolation plays (Figure 8-4a) are shown against a tight 62 defense. The shift is to flanker set to the shortside of an unbalanced line. Before we put these plays into application we will establish the following blocking assignments against the 62 defense shifted down one half a man.

1. *Split end*—Mirror block (set to the call).
2. *Tight end*—Seal block.
3. *Strongside tackles*—Lead block (call man).
4. *Strongside guards*—Post block.
5. *Center*—Outside gap (power rule).

6. *Shortside guards*—Outside gap (power rules).

7. *Shortside tackle*—Check and release (power rule).

Next we will show these two backside running plays run to the strongside of an unbalanced line:

1. *94 iso–split right* (Figure 8-4b). The tailback traps for the fullback who takes the hand-off through the 4 hole.

2. *95 iso–split left* (Figure 8-4c). The tailback traps for the fullback who takes the hand-off through the 5 hole.

On all tandem and isolation plays the quarterback bootlegs away from the call after he has handed off. He always checks out the backside for a possible bootleg pass. This will be covered in Chapter 12.

Next we will examine the isolation and tandem plays when they are used as a goal line offense.

USING IN SHORT YARDAGE SITUATIONS

We can project two kinds of short yardage situations. One is second or third down with two yards or less to go. The other is any time you are inside your own 5 yard line. We can predict 83, 65 or 56 goal line defenses. They all have one thing in common: they create gap situations. Our offense must become gap conscious in these situations. The offensive linemen must apply inside gap priority in their blocking rules.

We substitute a second tight end for our split end in short yardage situations. We use him as a seal blocker. It has been our experience that the unbalanced lines are more effective than the balanced line. This is because gap defenses have to shift down one full gap or leave a natural hole to the strongside. We obtain unbalanced lines through calling the tight ends to the calls on odd series and from the calls on even series. Our short yardage offense is made up of four basic plays featuring all three running backs. Running these four basic plays to both sides makes up a total eight plays. These plays are 60, 61, 76 and 77 tandems, plus 34, 35, 56 and 57 isolations. We call this our goal line offense or "Play the Game." This is also an excellent offense to use on a wet or muddy field.

Here is how we play the game between the offense and defense at the end of every practice when we are in pads. The ball is placed inside the 10 yard line and the offense is given four downs to score. The offense can only use the eight basic goal line plays. Both the first string offense vs. the first string defense and the second string offense vs. the second string defense have three fourth down opportunities. The teams that win two out of the three opportunities are dismissed from half of our wind sprints at the end of practice. This always generates much spirit and enthusiasm, even after a stale practice session. It also has a great carry-over value to game conditions.

Next we will show the eight basic goal line plays. The first four plays will be unbalanced right, and the second four plays will be unbalanced left. The first two plays will have the wingback set to the shortside of unbalanced lines, and the second two plays will be set to the strongside of unbalanced lines:

1. *61 tandem–tight right* (Figure 8-5) is shown against an 83 gap defense.

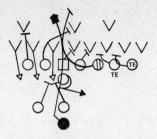

FIGURE 8-5: 61 TANDEM-TIGHT RIGHT

The left tackle and guard block and seal off the line of scrimmage. The center and right guard block outside gap. The right tackle pulls through the 1 hole. Both tight ends use cut-off blocks. The fullback and wing-back tandem the first down lineman to the left of center. The tailback takes the hand-off and carries the ball over center.

2. *76 tandem–tight right* (Figure 8-6) is run out of the same set as the 61 tandem. The call man back through center blocks the gaps. The outside tight end seals. The left guard pulls right through the hole. The fullback and tailback tandem the first defensive man to show outside of the 6 call man. The quarterback pivots and pitches to the wingback before leading him through the hole.

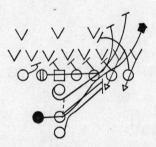

FIGURE 8-6: 76 TANDEM-TIGHT RIGHT

3. *34 iso–tight right* (Figure 8-7). The wingback is now set in the right half position to the strongside of an unbalanced line. The 4 call man back through the left guard blocks the gaps. The tight ends seal block. The fullback takes the hand-off through the hole to the inside of the wingback's trap.

4. *56 iso–tight right* (Figure 8-8) is run out of the same set as the 34 iso. The 6 call man back through the left guard blocks the gaps. The tight outside end seals. The tailback takes the hand-off and follows the full-back through the 6 hole to the inside of the wingback trap.

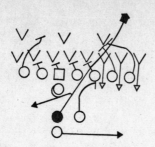

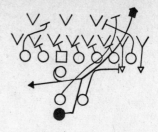

FIGURE 8-7: 34 ISO-TIGHT RIGHT

FIGURE 8-8: 56 ISO-TIGHT RIGHT

Next we look at these same 4 plays unbalanced to the left against 56 and 65 gap defenses.

1. *60 tandem–tight left* (Figure 8-9) is shown against a 65 goal line defense. The right tackle and guard block and seal off the line of scrimmage. The center blocks outside gap and the left guard the near linebacker. The left tackle pulls through the 1 hole. Both tight ends use cut-off blocks. The fullback and wingback tandem the first down lineman to the right of center. The tailback takes the hand-off and slides to the right of center.

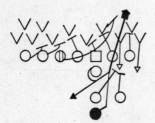

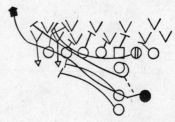

FIGURE 8-9: 60 TANDEM-TIGHT LEFT

FIGURE 8-10: 77 TANDEM-TIGHT LEFT

2. *77 tandem–tight left* (Figure 8-10) is run out of the same set as the 60 tandem. The 7 call man through center blocks the gaps or near linebackers in that order of priority. The right guard pulls left through the hole. The fullback and tailback tandem the first defensive man to show outside of the 7 call man. The quarterback pivots and pitches to the wingback before leading him through the hole.

3. *35 iso–tight left* (Figure 8-11). The wingback is now set in the left half position to the strongside of an unbalanced line. The defense is now in a 56 goal line defense. The 5 call man back through the right guard blocks the gaps or near linebackers in that order of priority. The tight ends seal blocks. The fullback takes the hand-off through the hole to the inside of the wingback trap.

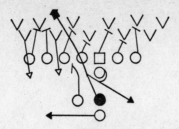

FIGURE 8-11: 35 ISO-TIGHT LEFT

4. *57 iso–tight left* (Figure 8-12) is run out of the same set as the 35 iso. The 7 call man back through the right guard blocks the gaps. The tight outside end seals. The tailback takes the hand-off and follows the full-back through the 7 hole to the inside of the wingback's trap.

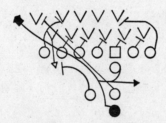

FIGURE 8-12: 57 ISO-TIGHT LEFT

Until now all but one play has been run from a fullhouse "I" backfield set. Next we will apply the shifts with our sweep, slant and reverse plays. Later we will again use the shifts with our passing and quick draw offense.

CHAPTER 9

Coaching Sweep-Slant
Plays in the
Multiple Power "I" Series

We have combined sweep and the outside trap techniques to get wide; the terms sweep and slant will be synonymous for us. The sweep plays will be applied with 8 and 9 holes, and the slant plays with 4, 5, 6 and 7 holes. The tailback will carry the ball on sweep plays; the fullback will carry it on slant plays. We have integrated both the lines blocking rules and the backfield techniques into one sequence. The sweep and slant plays have the same blocking schemes and backfield patterns. Our 4 and 5 slants will be applied to even series calls; 6 and 7 slants to odd series calls. This is because the tight end (6 or 7 call man) is set from the calls on even series. In addition to this we use the short reverse traps between a fake sweep-slant action. These plays are very deceptive: although they appear to be intricate, they are easy to teach and perfect in a limited amount of time.

Almost all of our plays up until now have been run from a fullhouse "I" backfield set. With sweep plays it is necessary to apply the shift to other sets. The following series calls will determine the shifts and sets.

1. *10-20 series* calls for a floater backfield set. The wingback shifts from his halfback position to a flanker set; the tailback shifts from his tailback position to a fullback set, and the fullback shifts to the backside halfback set. The sequence is run to the flanker side.

2. *90 series* calls for the same floater backfield set to the backside. The wingback sets and shifts from the call, and the fullback shifts to the call.

The same sweep-slant plays are run to the backside. These are the same sets from which we can run our 94 and 95 isolation plays.

3. *50-60 series* calls for a flanker or slot "I" backfield set. The wingback shifts from his halfback position to a flanker set to the call side.

We will use a four-phase format in two ways to illustrate our sweep techniques. First we will show the shifts and sequence patterns to both sides for each series. Second, we will show the multiple application for each series against an established defense. This will make it easy to understand.

THE 10, 20, 50 AND 60 FRONTSIDE SERIES

These are four frontside play sequences run to the flanker of slot side. Running them to both sides makes a total of eight sequences. Next we will show these four series in four phases:

The 10 series (Figure 9-1) is a two-play sweep-slant sequence run to the tight side of a balanced line or the strongside of an unbalanced line:

1. Figure 9-1a shows the shift on an even hole call to the right. The fullback shifts to the left half set. The tailback shifts into the fullback

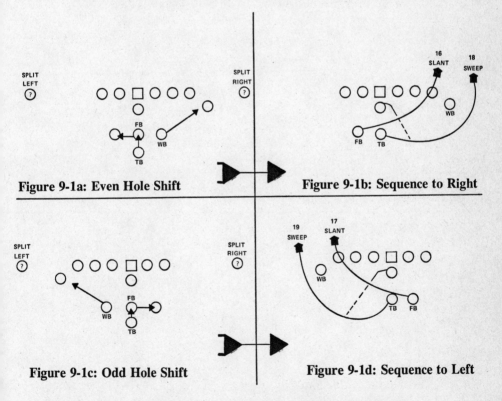

Figure 9-1a: Even Hole Shift

Figure 9-1b: Sequence to Right

Figure 9-1c: Odd Hole Shift

Figure 9-1d: Sequence to Left

FIGURE 9-1: 10 SERIES, SWEEP SLANT SEQUENCES

position. The wingback shifts from his right half position to a right flanker or slot set. This is a frontside shift to the right.

2. Figure 9-1b shows the two-play sequence run to the right. The quarterback takes a lead step to the right wiht a pitch-out motion to the tailback. On an 18 sweep the quarterback pitches to the tailback and keeps his hands extended for the fake of the fullback on the slant. On the 16 slant the quarterback uses exactly the same motion, but this time leaves the ball extended. The fullback takes the hand-off through the 6 hole.

3. Figure 9-1c shows the shift on an odd hole call to the left. The fullback shifts to the right half set. The tailback shifts into the fullback position. The wingback shifts from his left half position to a left flanker or slot set. This is a frontside shift to the left.

4. Figure 9-1d shows the two-play sequence run to the left. The quarterback lead steps to the left with a pitch out motion. On a 19 sweep he pitches to the tailback, and on 17 slant he leaves the ball extended for the fullback to take the hand-off.

The 20 series (Figure 9-2) is a two-play sweep-slant sequence run to the split side of a balanced line or the shortside of an unbalanced line.

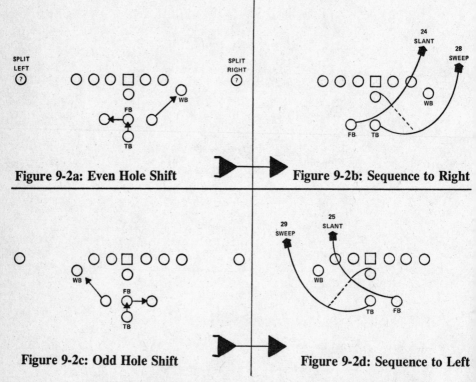

Figure 9-2a: Even Hole Shift

Figure 9-2b: Sequence to Right

Figure 9-2c: Odd Hole Shift

Figure 9-2d: Sequence to Left

FIGURE 9-2: 20 SERIES, SWEEP-SLANT SEQUENCES

1. Figure 9-2a shows the same backfield shift as was used in the 10 series to the right. The big difference is that the tight end is set to the left. This makes the right side either an unbalanced shortside with a flanker or a split side with a slot.

2. Figure 9-2b shows the same two-play sequence as in the 10 series run to the right. The difference is that the slant has to be moved in one full hole because there is no tight end to that side as a call man for the lead block. We make a 4 call instead of a 6 call. The quarterback makes no adjustments in his lead step and pitch out motion. The fullback must cut into the hole as soon as he receives the hand-off.

3. Figure 9-2c shows the same backfield shift as in the 10 series to the left. The difference is that the tight end is set to the right, making the right side either the shortside flanker to an unbalanced line or the split side of a slot.

4. Figure 9-2d shows the same two-play sequence as in the 10 series run to the left, except that the fullback's slant is now run through the 5 hole instead of the 7 hole.

Next we will show the sweep-slant sequence run from the 50-60 series. This calls for an "I" backfield set with only the wingback shifting to a flanker or slot. *The 50 series* (Figure 9-3) is the same as the 10 series except the sequence is

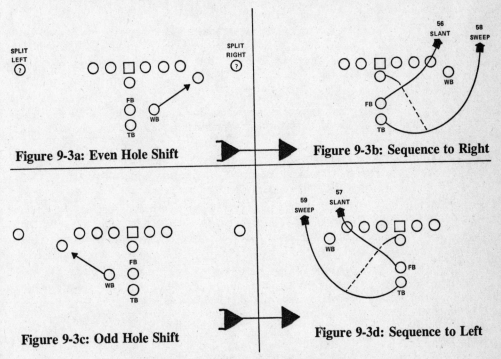

Figure 9-3a: Even Hole Shift

Figure 9-3b: Sequence to Right

Figure 9-3c: Odd Hole Shift

Figure 9-3d: Sequence to Left

FIGURE 9-3: 50 SERIES, SWEEP SLANT SEQUENCES

run from an "I" backfield set. It is run to the tight side of a balanced line or the strongside of an unbalanced line:

1. Figure 9-3a shows the shift on an even hole call to the right. The wingback is the only one in the backfield to shift. He shifts from his right half position to a right flanker or slot set. This is a frontside shift to the right.

2. Figure 9-3b shows the two-play sequence run to the right from an "I" set. The quarterback takes his lead step to the right with his pitch-out motion to the tailback. On a 58 sweep the quarterback pitches to the tailback and keeps his hands extended for the fake of the fullback on the slant. On the 56 slant the quarterback uses the same motion and leaves the ball extended for the fullback to take the hand-off through the 6 hole.

3. Figure 9-3c shows the solo shift of the wingback from his left half position to a left, flanker or slot set. This is a frontside shift to the left.

4. Figure 9-3d shows the two-play sequence run to the left from an "I" set. The quarterback takes his lead step to the left with his pitch-out motion to the tailback. On a 59 sweep the quarterback keeps his hands extended for the fullback fake slant after the pitch to the tailback. On the 57 slant the quarterback uses the same motion and leaves the ball extended for the fullback to take the hand off through the 7 hole.

The 60 series (Figure 9-4) is the same as the 20 except that the sequence is run from an "I" backfield set to the split or slot side of a balanced line and the short side of an unbalanced line. It differs from the 50 series in that the slants are moved one hole to the inside.

1. Figure 9-4a shows the same backfield shift as in the 50 series to the right. The difference is the tight end is set to the left, making the right side either an unbalanced shortside with a flanker or a split side with a slot.

2. Figure 9-4b shows the same two-play sequence and "I" set as in the 50 series run to the right. Because the tight end (6 call man) is set from the call, we make the fullback slant call at the 4 hole.

3. Figure 9-4c shows the same backfield shift as was in the 50 series to the left. The difference is the tight end is set to the right. This makes the left side either an unbalanced shortside with a flanker or a split side with a slot.

4. Figure 9-4d shows the same two-play sequence and "I" set as in the 50 series run to the left. Because the tight end (7 call man) is set from the call, we make the fullback slant call at the 5 hole.

This completes our frontside sweep-slant sequences. Next we will put each of these sequences into multiple application against a variety of defenses.

THE MULTIPLE APPLICATION OF THE FRONTSIDE SERIES

We will illustrate and explain the multiple application of each of the frontside sweep-slant sequences applied against eight different defenses. There will be

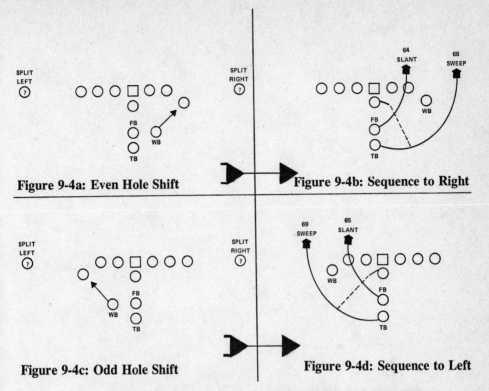

Figure 9-4a: Even Hole Shift

Figure 9-4b: Sequence to Right

Figure 9-4c: Odd Hole Shift

Figure 9-4d: Sequence to Left

FIGURE 9-4: 60 SERIES, SWEEP-SLANT SEQUENCES

four phases to each sequence. We will show the slant and sweep plays behind both balanced and unbalanced lines against the same defense in each sequence. This is done by simply flip-flopping our split end to give us a different situation against the same defense. It is easier to recognize and take advantage of multiple sets with sweep-slant plays than it was with our power or tandem plays. Now we will show the 10 and 20 series sequences which calls for a shift to a floater backfield set.

Figure 9-5 shows the *16 slant and 18 sweep* applied against a 52 monster defnese. We run this sequence behind both a balanced flanker to the right tightside and an unbalanced slot to the strongside right.

1. Before we put this sequence into multiple application we will establish the following blocking assignments that will be used against the *52 monster defense*:

   (1) *Right flanker*—16 slant—Inside near linebacker.
   18 sweep—Inside gap.

   (2) *Tight end*—Reach.

   (3) *Right tackle*—Near linebacker.

   (4) *Right guard*—16 slant—Pull right and trap.
   18 sweep—Pull right and seal.

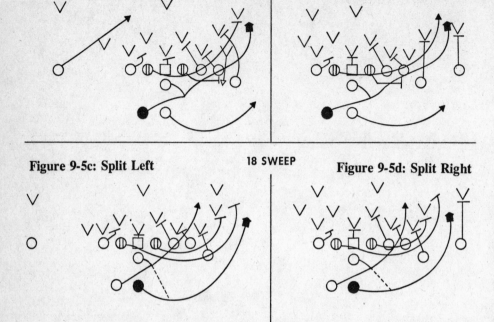

Figure 9-5a: Split Left 16 SLANT **Figure 9-5b: Split Right**

Figure 9-5c: Split Left 18 SWEEP **Figure 9-5d: Split Right**

FIGURE 9-5: 16-18 MULTIPLE APPLICATION VS. 52 MONSTER

(5) *Center*—On.

(6) *Left guard*—Pull right and seal.

(7) *Left tackle*—Cut-off.

(8) *Split end*—Set right—Mirror block.
　　　　　　　　 Set left—Release to Baker.

2. *Multiple application of 16 slant* (Figure 9-5). The quarterback lead steps to the right with a pitch-out motion and leaves the ball extended for the fullback to take the hand-off through the 6 hole.

   Figure 9-5a. When the split end is set to the left, we run 16 slant to the tight side of a balanced line.

   Figure 9-5b. When the split end is set to the right, we run 16 slant to the strongside of an unbalanced line.

3. *Multiple application of 18 sweep* (Figure 9-5). The quarterback lead steps to the right and pitches to the tailback leaving his hands extended for the fullback to fake his slant through the 6 hole.

   Figure 9-5c. When the split end is set to the left, we run 18 sweep to the flanker side of a balanced line.

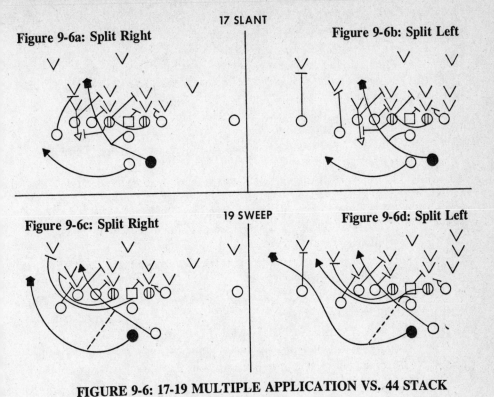

17 SLANT

Figure 9-6a: Split Right   **Figure 9-6b: Split Left**

Figure 9-6c: Split Right   **19 SWEEP**   **Figure 9-6d: Split Left**

FIGURE 9-6: 17-19 MULTIPLE APPLICATION VS. 44 STACK

Figure 9-5d. When the split end is set to the right, we run 18 sweep to the slot side of an unbalanced line.

Figure 9-6 shows the *17 slant and 19 sweep* applied against a 44 stack defense. We run this sequence behind both a balanced flanker to the left tight side and an unbalanced slot to the strongside left.

1. Before we put this sequence into multiple application we will establish the following blocking assignments that will be used against the *44 stack defense*:

   (1) *Left flanker*—17 slant—Inside near linebacker.
                          19 sweep—Reach.

   (2) *Tight end*—Inside near linebacker.

   (3) *Left tackle*—Reach.

   (4) *Left guard*—17 slant—Pull left and trap.
                      19 sweep—Pull left and seal.

   (5) *Center*—Reach.

   (6) *Right guard*—Pull left and seal.

(7) *Right tackle*—Cut-off.

(8) *Split end*—Set left—Mirror block.
   Set right—Release to Baker.

2. *Multiple application of 17 slant* (Figure 9-6). The quarterback lead steps to the left wiht a pitch-out motion and leaves the ball extended for the fullback to take the hand-off through the 7 hole.

Figure 9-6a. When the split end is set to the right, we run 17 slant to the tight side of a balanced line.

Figure 9-6b. When the split end is set to the left, we run 17 slant to the strongside of an unbalanced line.

3. *Mutliple application of 19 sweep* (Figure 9-6). The quarterback lead steps to the left and pitches to the tailback, leaving his hand extended for the fullback to fake his slant through the 7 hole.

Figure 9-6c. When the split end is set to the right, we run 19 sweep to the flanker side of a balanced line.

Figure 9-6d. When the split end is set to the left, we run 19 sweep to the slot side of an unbalanced line.

Figure 9-7 shows the *24 slant and 28 sweep* applied against a split 62 defense. We run this sequence behind both a balanced slot to the right split side and an unbalanced flanker to the short side right.

   1. Before we put this sequence into multiple application we will establish the following blocking assignments that will be used against the *split 62 defense*:

(1) *Right flanker*—24 slant—Inside near linebacker.
      28 sweep—Inside gap.

(2) *Right tackle*—Inside gap.

(3) *Right guard*—24 slant—Pull right and influence.
      28 sweep—Pull right and seal.

(4) *Center*—Near linebacker.

(5) *Left guard*—24 slant—Pull right and trap.
      28 sweep—Pull right and seal.

(6) *Left tackle*—Cut-off.

(7) *Tight end*—Cut-off.

(8) *Split end*—Set right—Mirror block.
      Set left—Release to Baker.

2. *Multiple application of 24 slant* (Figure 9-7). The quarterback lead steps to the right with a pitch-out motion and leaves the ball extended for the fullback to take the hand-off through the 4 hole.

Figure 9-7a. When the split end is set to the right, we run 24 slant to the split side of a balanced line.

Figure 9-7b. When the split end is set to the left, we run 24 slant to the short side of an unbalanced line.

24 SLANT

Figure 9-7a: Split Right   **Figure 9-7b: Split Left**

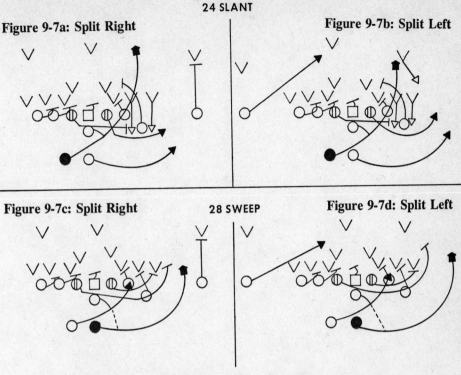

Figure 9-7c: Split Right   **28 SWEEP**   **Figure 9-7d: Split Left**

FIGURE 9-7: MULTIPLE APPLICATION VS. SPLIT 62

   3. *Multiple application of 28 sweep* (Figure 9-7). The quarterback lead steps to the right and pitches to the tailback leaving his hand extended for the fullback to fake his hand-off through the 4 hole.

   Figure 9-7c. When the split end is set to the right, we run 28 sweep to the slot side of a balanced line.

   Figure 9-7d. When the split end is set to the left, we run 28 sweep to the flanker shortside of an unbalanced line.

   Figure 9-8 shows *25 slant and 29 sweep* applied against a 44 stack defense. We run this sequence behind both a balance slot to the left split side and an unbalanced flanker to the shortside left.

   1. Before we put this sequence into multiple application we will establish the following blocking assignments that will be used against the *44 stack defense*:

      (1) *Left flanker*—25 slant—Inside near linebacker.
                        29 sweep—Inside gap.

      (2) *Left tackle*—Reach.

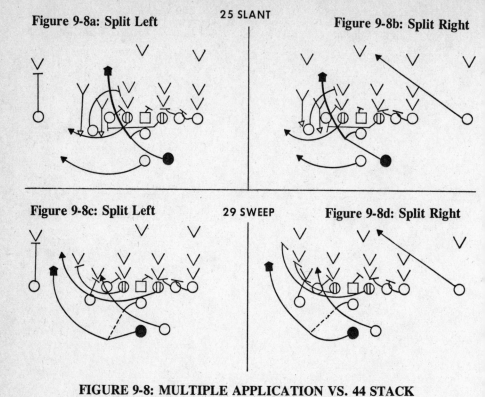

FIGURE 9-8: MULTIPLE APPLICATION VS. 44 STACK

   (3) *Left guard*—25 slant—Pull left and influence.
                   29 sweep—Pull left and seal.

   (4) *Center*—Reach.

   (5) *Right guard*—25 slant—Pull left and trap.
                   29 sweep—Pull left and seal.

   (6) *Right tackle*—Cut-off.

   (7) *Tight end*—Cut-off.

   (8) *Split end*—Set left (mirror block).
                 Set right—Release to Baker.

  2. *Multiple application of 25 slant* (Figure 9-8). The quarterback lead steps to the left with a pitch-out motion and leaves the ball extended for the fullback to take the hand-off through the 5 hole.

    Figure 9-8a. When the split end is set to the left, we run 25 slant to the split side of a balanced line.

    Figure 9-8b. When the split end is set to the right, we run 25 slant to the shortside of an unbalanced line.

3. *Multiple application of 29 sweep* (Figure 9-8). The quarterback lead steps to the left and pitches to the tailback leaving his hands extended for the fullback to fake his hand-off through the 5 hole.

Figure 9-8c. When the split end is set to the left, we run 29 sweep to the slot side of a balanced line.

Figure 9-8d. When the split end is set to the right, we run 29 sweep to the flanker shortside of an unbalanced line.

Next we will run these same four sequences from an "I" backfield set against an additional variation of defenses. The 50 series sequences will be the same as the 10 series and the 60 series sequences will be the same as the 20 series. The only difference will be in the backfield set. In the 10 and 20 series the fullback ran his slants from a backside halfback set, and the tailback ran his sweeps from the fullback set. With the 50 and 60 series the tailback and fullback will both run their slants and sweeps from their basic "I" sets without a shift. Though the offense is still doing the same thing, it looks very different from a defense's point of view. We have found the same play to be more effective out of one backfield set than it had been out of another. This varies depending on the characteristics of the opposing team and the tendencies of the defense. The same question arises on the question of whether the slant sets up the sweep or the sweep sets up the slant. What difference does it make which came first—the chicken or the egg? What is important is that one is dependent on the other. With the sweep-slant sequence we only know that if one doesn't work the other one will. After we get one to work it will lead to making the other one work.

Figure 9-9 shows the *56 slant and 58 sweep* applied against a 43 invert defense. We run this sequence behind both a balanced flanker to the right tight side and an unbalanced slot to the strongside right.

1. Before we put this sequence into multiple application we will establish the following blocking assignments that will be used against the *43 invert defense*:

   (1) *Right flanker*—56 slant—Inside near linebacker.
                   58 sweep—Reach.

   (2) *Tight end*—Inside linebacker.

   (3) *Right tackle*—Reach.

   (4) *Right guard*—56 slant—Pull right and trap.
                 58 sweep—Pull right and seal.

   (5) *Center*—Near linebacker.

   (6) *Left guard*—Pull right and seal.

   (7) *Left tackle*—Cut-off.

   (8) *Split end*—Set right—Mirror block.
                 Set left—Release to Baker.

2. *Multiple application of 56 slant* (Figure 9-9). The quarterback lead steps to the right with a pitch-out motion and leaves the ball extended for the fullback to take the hand-off through the 6 hole.

Figure 9-9a. When the split end is set to the left, we run 56 slant to the tight side of a balanced line.

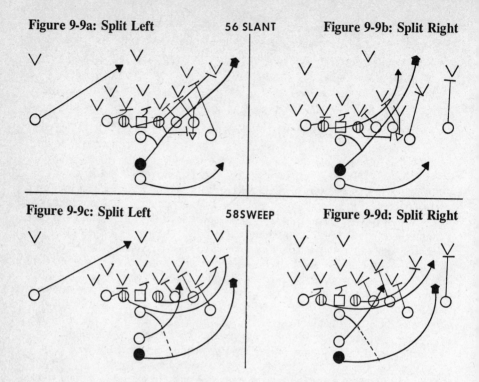

FIGURE 9-9: 56-58 MULTIPLE APPLICATION VS. 43 INVERT

Figure 9-9b. When the split end is set to the right, we run 56 slant to the strongside of an unbalanced line.

3. *Multiple application of 58 sweep* (Figure 9-9). The quarterback lead steps to the right and pitches to the tailback, leaving his hands extended for the fullback to fake his slant through the 6 hole.

Figure 9-9c. When the split end is set to the left, we run 58 sweep to the flanker side of a balanced line.

Figure 9-9d. When the split end is set to the right, we run 58 sweep to the slot side of an unbalanced line.

Figure 9-10 shows the *57 slant and 59 sweep* applied against an eagle 53 defense. We run this sequence behind both a balanced flanker to the left tight side nad an unbalanced slot to the strongside left.

1. Before we put this sequence into application we will establish the following blocking assignments that will be used against the *eagle 53 defense*.

   (1) *Left flanker*—57 slant—Near linebacker.
   59 sweep—Inside gap.

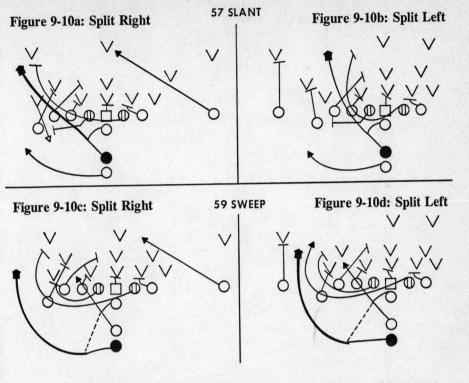

FIGURE 9-10: 57-59 MULTIPLE APPLICATION VS. EAGLE 53

(2) *Tight end*—Inside near linebacker.

(3) *Left tackle*—Inside gap.

(4) *Left guard*—57 slant—Pull left and trap.
            59 sweep—Pull left and seal.

(5) *Center*—On.

(6) *Right guard*—Pull left and seal.

(7) *Right tackle*—Cut-off.

(8) *Split end*—Set left (mirror block).
            Set right—Release to Baker.

2. *Multiple application of 57 slant* (Figure 9-10). The quarterback lead steps to the left with a pitch-out motion and leaves the ball extended for the fullback to take the hand-off through the 7 hole.

Figure 9-10a. When the split end is set to the right, we run 57 slant to the tight side of a balanced line.

Figure 9-10b. When the split end is set to the left, we run 57 slant to the strongside of an unbalanced line.

3. *Multiple application of 59 sweep* (Figure 9-10). The quarterback lead steps to the left and pitches to the tailback, leaving his hands extended for the fullback to fake his slant through the 7 hole.

Figure 9-10c. When the split end is set to the right, we run 59 sweep to the flanker side of a balanced line.

Figure 9-10d. When the split end is set to the left, we run 59 sweep to the slot side of an unbalanced line.

Figure 9-11 shows the *64 slant and 68 sweep* applied against a split 44 defense. We run this sequence behind both a balanced slot to the right split side and an unbalanced flanker to the short side right.

1. Before we put this sequence into multiple application we will establish the following blocking assignments that will be used against the *split 44 defense*.

  (1) *Right flanker*—64 slant—Inside near linebacker.
       68 sweep—Inside gap.

  (2) *Right tackle*—Inside gap.

  (3) *Right guard*—64 slant—Pull right and influence.
       68 sweep—Pull right and seal.

  (4) *Center*—Near linebacker.

  (5) *Left guard*—64 slant—Pull right and trap.
       68 sweep—Pull right and seal.

  (6) *Left tackle*—Cut-off.

  (7) *Tight end*—Cut-off.

  (8) *Split end*—Set right (mirror block).
       Set left—Release to Baker.

2. *Multiple application of 64 slant* (Figure 9-11). The quarterback lead steps to the right with a pitch-out motion and leaves the ball extended for the fullback to take the hand-off through the 4 hole.

Figure 9-11a. When the split end is set to the right, we run 64 slant to the split side of a balanced line.

Figure 9-11b. When the split end is set to the left, we run 64 slant to the shortside of an unbalanced line.

3. *Multiple application of 68 sweep* (Figure 9-11). The quarterback lead steps to the right and pitches to the tailback, leaving his hand extended for the fullback to fake his hand-off through the 4 hole.

Figure 9-11c. When the split end is set to the right, we run 68 sweep to the slot side of a balanced line.

Figure 9-11d. When the split end is set to the left, we run 68 sweep to the flanker shortside of an unbalanced line.

Figure 9-12 shows *65 slant and 69 sweep* applied against a wide tackle 62 defense. We run this sequence behind both a balanced slot to the left split side and an unbalanced flanker to the shortside left.

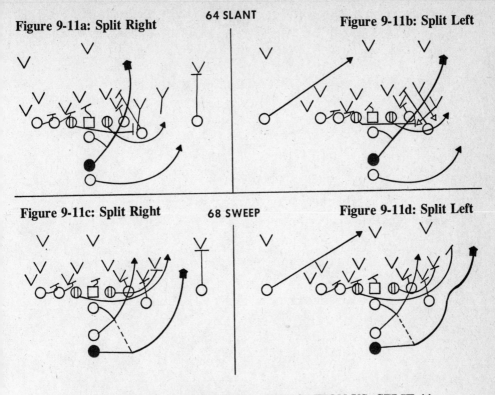

64 SLANT

Figure 9-11a: Split Right

Figure 9-11b: Split Left

Figure 9-11c: Split Right   **68 SWEEP**

Figure 9-11d: Split Left

FIGURE 9-11: 64-68 MULTIPLE APPLICATION VS. SPLIT 44

1. Before we put this sequence into multiple application we will establish the following blocking assignments that will be used against a *wide tackle 62 defense*:

    (1) *Left flanker*—65 slant—Inside near linebacker.
                 69 sweep—Inside gap.

    (2) *Left tackle*—Reach.

    (3) *Left guard*—65 slant—Pull left and influence.
               69 sweep—Pull left and seal.

    (4) *Center*—Reach.

    (5) *Right guard*—65 slant—Pull left and trap.
                69 sweep—Pull left and seal.

    (6) *Right tackle*—Cut-off.

    (7) *Tight end*—Cut-off.

    (8) *Split end*—Set left (mirror block).
              Set right—Release to Baker.

Figure 9-12a: Split Left 65 SLANT **Figure 9-12b: Split Right**

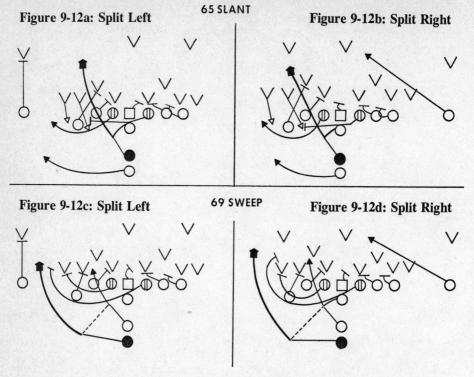

Figure 9-12c: Split Left 69 SWEEP **Figure 9-12d: Split Right**

FIGURE 9-12: 65-69 MULTIPLE APPLICATION VS. WIDE TACKLE 62

2. *Multiple application of 65 slant* (Figure 9-12). The quarterback lead steps to the left with a pitch-out motion and leaves the ball extended for the fullback to take the hand-off through the 5 hole.

Figure 9-12a. When the split end is set to the left, we run 65 slant to the split side of a balanced line.

Figure 9-12b. When the split end is set to the right, we run 65 slant to the shortside of an unbalanced line.

3. *Multiple application of 69 sweep* (Figure 9-12). The quarterback lead steps to the left and pitches to the tailback, leaving his hands extended for the fullback to fake his hand-off through the 5 hole.

Figure 9-12c. When the split end is set to the left, we run 69 sweep to the slot side of a balanced line.

Figure 9-12d. When the split end is set to the right, we run 69 sweep to the flanker shortside of an unbalanced line.

This completes our sweep-slant plays to the frontside. We have two ways of attacking the backside. First we will show our 90 backside series; second, we will integrate the reverses with the sweep-slant sequences that we use in our frontside attack. The wingback carries the ball on all slants and reverses to the backside.

CHAPTER 10

Utilizing Backside
Sweep-Slant Plays
and Reverses

THE BACKSIDE 90 SERIES

The 90 series has the same play sequence, shifts and backfield sets to the backside as the 10 and 20 series to the frontside. The fullback shifts to the halfback set to the call; the tailback shifts to the fullback set. The wingback shifts from his halfback set to a flanker set from the call, and the wingback takes the hand-offs on the slants. This gives us the basic sweep-slant sequences to the backside.

The 90 series (Figure 10-1) is a two-play sweep slant sequence run to the tight side of a balanced line or the strongside of an unbalanced line.

1. Figure 10-1a shows the shift on an even hole call to the right. The fullback shifts to the right half set. The tailback shifts into the fullback position, and the wingback shifts from his left half position to a left flanker or slot set. This is a backside shift to the right.

2. Figure 10-1b shows the two-play sequence run to the right. The quarterback takes a lead step to the right wiht a pitch-out motion to the tailback. On a 98 sweep the quarterback pitches out to the tailback and leaves his hands extended for the fake of the wingback on the slant. On 96 slant the quarterback uses the same motion, but this time leaves the ball extended. The wingback takes the hand-off through the 6 hole.

3. Figure 10-1c shows the shift on an odd hole call to the left. The fullback shifts to a left half set. The tailback shifts into the fullback position. The

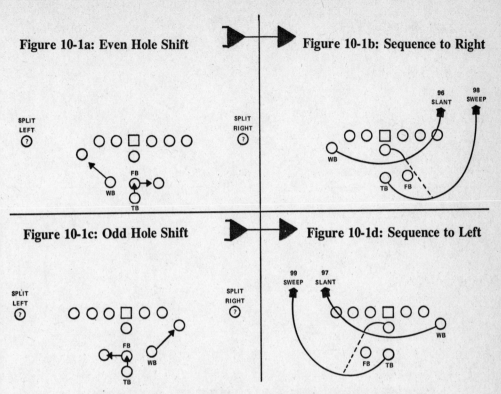

Figure 10-1a: Even Hole Shift

Figure 10-1b: Sequence to Right

Figure 10-1c: Odd Hole Shift

Figure 10-1d: Sequence to Left

FIGURE 10-1: 90 SERIES, SWEEP-SLANT SEQUENCES

wingback shifts from his right half position to a right flanker or slot set. This is a backside shift to the left.

4. Figure 10-1d shows the two-play sequence run to the left. The quarterback takes a lead step to the left with a pitch-out motion to the tailback. On a 99 sweep the quarterback pitches to the tailback and keeps his hands extended for the fake of the wingback on the slant. On 97 slant the quarterback uses the same motion, but this time leaves the ball extended. The wingback takes the hand-off through the 7 hole.

Now we will show the multiple application of the 90 series.

THE MULTIPLE APPLICATION OF
THE BACKSIDE SERIES

We run the 90 sweep-slant sequence to the tight side of a balanced line, or the strongside of an unbalanced line. If we felt a need to run this sequence to the split side of a balanced line or the short side of an unbalanced line, we could simply call it from the 100 series. We do not use the 100 series because the

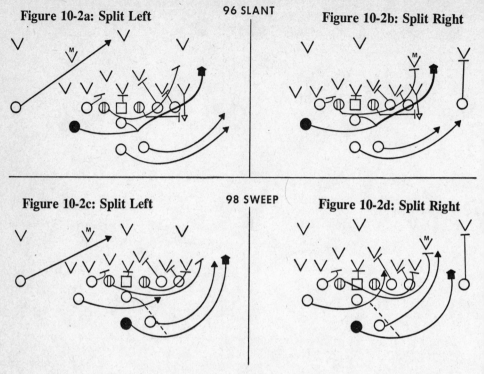

FIGURE 10-2: 96-98 MULTIPLE APPLICATION VS. 52 MONSTER

timing is not natural for the wingback to carry the ball into the 4 or 5 hole on a slant. With even series calls we can not make 6 or 7 hole calls because the tight end is set from the call. The wingback's timing is right on a 6 or 7 slant from the 90 series. The 90 series formations are the same as the 20 series formations. To get multiple sets of the 90 series we call the split end from the call to get balanced lines and to the call to get unbalanced lines.

Figure 10-2 shows the *96 slant and 98 sweep* applied against a 52 monster defense. The monster is set to the wingback side; we will attack the side away from him. We run this sequence to the right tight side of a balanced line or strongside right of an unbalanced line.

1. Before we put this sequence into application we will establish the following blocking assignments that we will use against the *52 monster defense*:

   (1) *Tight end*—Inside gap.

   (2) *Right tackle*—Inside near linebacker.

   (3) *Right guard*—96 slant—Pull right and trap.

                         98 sweep—Pull right and lead.

   (4) *Center*—On.

(5) *Left guard*—Pull right and seal.

(6) *Left tackle*—Cut-off.

(7) *Split end*—Set right (mirror block).
     Set left—Release to Baker.

2. *Multiple application of 96 slant* (Figure 10-2). The quarterback lead steps to the right with a pitch-out motion and leaves the ball extended for the wingback to take the ball through the 6 hole.

Figure 10-2a. When the split end is set to the left, we run 96 slant to the tight side of a balanced line from the monster.

Figure 10-2b. When the split end is set to the right, we run 96 slant to the strongside of an unbalanced line toward the monster.

3. *Multiple application of 98 sweep* (Figure 10-2). The quarterback lead steps to the right and pitches to the tailback, leaving his hands extended for the wingback to fake his slant through the 6 hole.

Figure 10-2c. When the split end is set to the left, we run 98 sweep to the tight side of a balanced line from the monster.

Figure 10-2d. When the split end is set to the right, we run 98 sweep to the strongside of an unbalanced line toward the monster.

Figure 10-3 shows the *97 slant and 99 sweep* applied against a 44 stack defense. The fullback leads the tailback on the sweep, and the wingback carries the ball on the slant. We run the sequence to the left tight side of a balanced line or strongside left of an unbalanced line.

1. Before we put this sequence into application we will establish the following blocking assignments that we will use against the *44 stack defense*.

(1) *Tight end*—Inside linebacker.

(2) *Left tackle*—Reach.

(3) *Left guard*—97 slant—Pull left and trap.
     99 sweep—Pull left and lead.

(4) *Center*—Reach near linebacker.

(5) *Right guard*—Pull left and seal.

(6) *Right tackle*—Cut-off.

(7) *Split end*—Set left (mirror block).
     Set right—Release to Baker.

2. *Multiple application of 97 slant* (Figure 10-3). The quarterback lead steps to the left with a pitch-out motion, and leaves the ball extended for the wingback to take the hand-off through the 7 hole.

Figure 10-3a. When the split end is set to the right, we run 97 slant to the tight side of a balanced line.

Figure 10-3b. When the split end is set to the left, we run 97 slant to the strongside of an unbalanced line.

3. *Multiple application of 99 sweep* (Figure 10-3). The quarterback lead

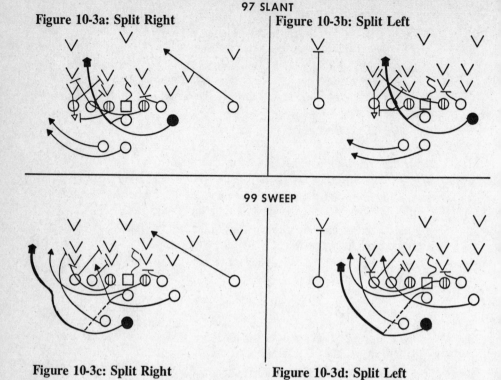

97 SLANT

Figure 10-3a: Split Right

Figure 10-3b: Split Left

99 SWEEP

Figure 10-3c: Split Right

Figure 10-3d: Split Left

FIGURE 10-3: 97-99 MULTIPLE APPLICATION VS. 44 STACK

steps to the left and pitches to the tailback, leaving his hands extended for the wingback to fake his slant through the 7 hole.

Figure 10-3c. When the split end is set to the right, we run 99 sweep to the tight side of a balanced line.

Figure 10-3d. When the split end set to the left, we run 99 sweep to the strongside of an unbalanced line.

This completes our basic sweep-slant techniques to both the frontside and backside. Next we will integrate the short inside reverse into the frontside sweep-slant pattern. This is a backside play in which we will increase the sequence to a three-play pattern.

INTEGRATING THE REVERSES WITH
THE FRONTSIDE SERIES

Most coaches are familiar with the inside reverse after a fake dive to the halfback or fullback. We have discovered that it will break faster if you fake the sweep instead. This is very effective after you have run a number of successful

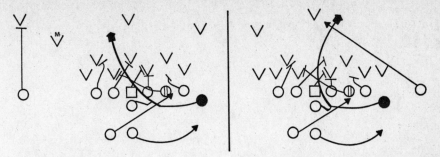

Figure 10-4a: 21 Reverse, Split Left   **Figure 10-4b: 21 Reverse, Split Right**

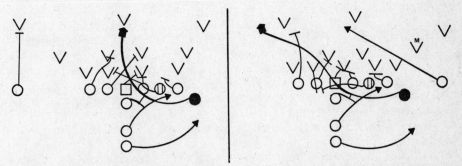

Figure 10-4c: 61 Reverse, Split Left   **Figure 10-4d: 61 Reverse, Split Right**

FIGURE 10-4: MULTIPLE APPLICATION OF 1 AND 0 REVERSE VS. EVEN DEFENSES

sweeps and slants. The quarterback lead steps toward the wingback with a pitch-out motion to the tailback. The wingback heads directly to where the ball was set before the snap. The quarterback makes an inside hand-off to him behind his trapping tackle. After the quarterback hands off he extends his hands for the fake of the fullback on the slant.

We use 0 and 1 trap (tandem rules) blocking with our reverse calls. The reverses work better against even defenses than they do against odd ones. On even defenses the center is the lead man; on odd defenses the guards are the lead men. We will show one sequence of reverses against a variety of even defenses and another sequence of reverses against odd defenses. With reverses we only use even series call because we want the tight ends set from the call. We need his cut-off block for our pulling and trapping tackles.

Figure 10-4 shows the multiple application of "I" reverses against a variation of even defenses. First we will establish their following blocking assignments:

(1) *Left tackle*—Near linebacker.

(2) *Left guard*—Seal.

(3) *Center*—Lead (call man)

(4) *Right guard*—Post.

(5) *Right tackle*—Pull left and trap.

(6) *Tight end*—Cut off.

(7) *Split end*—Set left (mirror block).
       Set right—Release to Baker.

Figure 10-4a shows a 21 reverse being run against a 43 defense. The split end is called to the left to give a balanced line in front of a floater "T" backfield set.

Figure 10-4b shows a 21 reverse being run against a wide tackle 62 defense. The split end is called to the right to give an unbalanced line to the strongside of a floater "T" backfield set.

Figure 10-4c shows a 61 reverse being run against a 44 stack defense. The split end is called to the left to give a flanker "I" backfield set behind a balanced line.

Figure 10-4d shows a 61 reverse being run against a 52 monster defense shifted down one half of a man. This makes it an even defense. The split end is called to the right to give a slot "I" backfield set to the strongside of an unbalanced line.

Figure 10-5 shows the multiple application of "0" reverses against odd defenses. We will first show an even defense and then shift it down one full man to change it to an odd defense. We will establish the following blocking assignments against odd defenses:

(1) *Right tackle*—Seal.

(2) *Right guard*—Lead (call man)

(3) *Center*—Post.

(4) *Left guard*—Apply power rules.

(5) *Left tackle*—Pull right and trap.

(6) *Tight end*—Cut off.

(7) *Split end*—Set right (mirror block).
       Set left—Release to Baker.

Figure 10-5a shows a 20 reverse being run against a 43 defense. (Apply blocking assignments vs. even defenses). The split end is called to the right to give a balanced line in front of a floater "T" backfield set.

Figure 10-5b shows a 20 reverse being run against a 43 defense shifted down one full man. This changes it to an odd defense. The split end is called to the left to give an unbalanced line to the strongside of a floater backfield set.

Figure 10-5c shows a 60 reverse being run against a 52 monster defense. The monster is playing the wingback side. The split end is called to the right to give a flanker "I" backfield set behind a balanced line.

Figure 10-5d shows a 60 reverse being run against a tight 62 defense shifted to our strongside one full man. This makes it an odd defense. The split end is

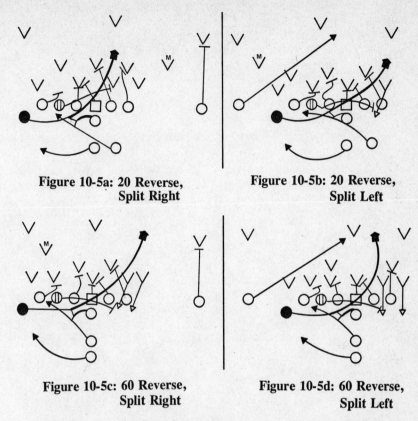

Figure 10-5a: 20 Reverse, Split Right

Figure 10-5b: 20 Reverse, Split Left

Figure 10-5c: 60 Reverse, Split Right

Figure 10-5d: 60 Reverse, Split Left

FIGURE 10-5: MULTIPLE APPLICATION OF 0 REVERSE VS. ODD DEFENSES

called to the left to give a slot "I" backfield set to the strongside of an unbalanced line.

This completes our basic running attack from the multiple power "I" system. In conclusion we will review this running attack with the elimination of the multiple formations. This will give us a final analysis of how simple this offense is. This running attack has been in three phases; the power sequence and sweep sequence each have three basic plays. The tandem techniques had four basic plays. All of these plays being run out of a single set to both sides is a sum total of 20 running plays. In the teaching and learning of this offense, we concentrate only on these 20 plays. Only after they are perfected to our satisfaction do we consider multiple application. This is only the second part of the multiple aspect. The other part of multiple application, integrating and combining the different techniques and tactical characteristics, is probably more important to you than our multiple sets. This is because you can integrate many of our ideas into your system, but in many cases to use our approach for multiple sets you would have to change your system. This could not be considered practical. We have all seen one team be highly successful and another team be a total failure using the same system. People make the system: the system does not make people. What is the most important is not the system but its related techniques which can be applied to your system. There is such a cross section of integrated ideas combined into these 20 plays that at least some of the following ideas will apply to your situation:

1. If you run a triple option sequence you should be interested in the additional multiple application.
2. If you run an "I" system you should be interested in the integration of our techniques.
3. Regardless of your system, you use either the sweep, slant or inside reverse. We have combined all three plays into one sequence of backfield patterns. This in itself should be of interest to you.

Not even our quarterbacks realize that we are able to make over 600 calls with the multiple application of these 20 basic running plays. We don't want them to be concerned with this but only to concentrate on the 20 basic plays and the sets only as we need and use them.

Next we must have a passing attack to complement these 20 basic running plays. We will use play action passes that are related to our power techniques and bootleg passes that are related to our tandem techniques. We also use series of slots and flankers with no faking so we can get a fourth receiver into our patterns. The following two chapters will cover our complementary passing system and its multiple application.

CHAPTER 11

Integrating the Multiple Power "I" Passing System

Only recently have we put much emphasis on our passing game. As a team, we had a reputation of being conservative and dependent on a strong running attack. From a defensive point of view, this left a weak tendency. The defense knew if we scored first we could control the ball, but if the opposition scored first we were forced to do things that we did not like to do: it put us in a position where we would make the mistakes. We have reversed this tendency. During recent years we have never been beaten as a result of a turnover from a pass interception. In the course of a season, we will have more turnovers from fumbles than we do from interceptions. This has not been an accident. We spend almost as much time practicing our passing game as we do our running game, and we average putting the ball in the air 20 percent of the time per season. During this period, our passers had a 54 percent completion average. We are not concerned that we have averaged only seven touchdown passes a year. Because of zone coverages we don't throw the bomb. Most of the time our passing has moved the ball down inside the 10 yard line to set-up a score from a running play.

We have all heard the quote, "When you throw the football three things can happen—and two of them are bad!" The one good thing is a completion; the two bad ones are an incompletion with the loss of a down, and a turnover through an interception. If we can eliminate the interceptions and complete more than half of our passes, the good will far out-weigh the bad.

Another quote that has had an influence on our passing system is "Pass short for go, and long for show." The short pass can be a high percentage play;

the long pass is a low percentage play. Our passing objective is to throw short without an interception. This makes it a low risk play. We will throw the bomb only if it is given to us. This does not happen very often because we see more zone than man-to-man coverages.

TECHNIQUES OF THE PASSERS AND RECEIVERS

Our passing techniques are based on keying a defensive back with a priority for receivers in mind. Our passer is trained to throw where the defensive man is not, and it is the responsibility of the receiver to be there. This is done by cutting two receivers in different directions off one defensive back. Before we can key the defensive back we need to establish the following order of priorities for receivers (Figure 11-1):

    1. *Primary targets;*
       First priority—Tight receiver to the call.
       Second priority—Split receiver to the call.

    2. *Secondary targets;*
       Third priority—A fourth receiver releases from the backfield to a zone.
       Fourth priority—The end set from the call.

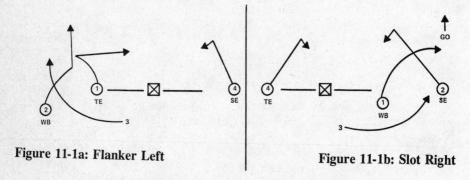

Figure 11-1a: Flanker Left   **Figure 11-1b: Slot Right**

FIGURE 11-1: ORDER OF PRIORITIES

Our primary targets are to the call. They are made up of the two receivers who have first and second priorities. The first priority is the tight receiver to the call. He can either be a wingback set in a slot or the tight end set in a wide flanker pro-set. He must receive the ball on his cut. The second priority receiver is either the split end in a slot or the wingback set as a wide flanker. Our secondary targets are our third and fourth priority receivers. The third priority receiver is a back who is released out of the backfield to the primary zone after the two primary receivers have cleared out. The fourth priority is the end set from the call and has been predetermined as a receiver after being ignored by the defense.

Figure 11-2 shows the keying of the defensive fifth man (Chapter 4, Figure 4-7). He can be a corner back, monster or pre-rotated invert. Regardless of his name or responsibilities, he is the first outside defensive back off the line of scrimmage to the outside of our offensive tackle. The wingback in a slot set has

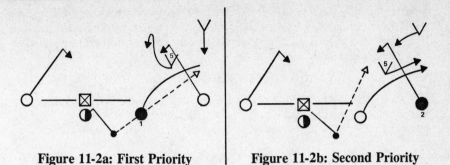

| Figure 11-2a: First Priority | Figure 11-2b: Second Priority |

FIGURE 11-2: KEYING PRIMARY TARGETS

first priority as a primary receiver (Figure 11-2a). He cuts in front of the fifth defensive man. If the fifth man doesn't cover him, the quarterback must hit him on the cut. The tight end has the second priority as a primary receiver (Figure 11-2b). He hooks in behind the fifth man. If the fifth man covers the wingback, the quarterback hits the tight end.

Figure 11-3 shows the keying of the defensive half if both primary receivers are covered (Figure 11-3a). When the quarterback fakes with a pump, this is a key for his primary receivers to break on their secondary routes. The defensive half is the quarterback's secondary key. On the pump the wingback sprints straight down the field which results in a staircase pattern. The quarterback fades three more steps and throws the ball with a high arch beyond the reach of the defensive half. It is up to the wingback to run under it. If the defensive half has recovered deep, the quarterback looks for the third priority receiver in the short zone that has been left cleared out by the primary receivers. The receiver with third priority can either be out of the backfield or the hook receiver in his secondary route if a fake was called in the backfield. The fourth priority is always

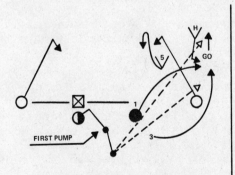

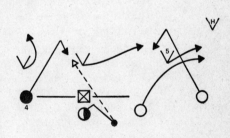

| Figure 11-3a: Third Priority | Figure 11-3b: Fourth Priority |

FIGURE 11-3: KEYING SECONDARY TARGETS

predetermined (Figure 11-3b). If the end from the call is left uncovered, he then tells the quarterback before the huddle and becomes a primary receiver. This is a short back side pass. Basically all of our primary targets are short passes and all of our secondary targets are long passes.

THE ZONES

Our zones were covered in Chapter 1 (Figure 1-4). The short zones for primary targets are Dog and Easy. Dog is to the right and Easy is to the left. Our three deep zones for secondary target are Able, Baker and Charlie.

THE METHOD OF CALLING

We use the same method for calling pass plays that we did for our running plays but with the elimination of the second word. This is because the set of our split end is predetermined by the same method our tight end uses on running plays. On odd series the tight end sets to the call and the split end sets from the call. On even series the split end sets to the call and the tight end sets from the call. This has eliminated our unbalanced lines from our passing system. If we should feel a need to pass from an unbalanced line, we would simply add the second word in our calls as we do with our running plays.

This leaves our method for calling plays in three parts. We use two digits followed by one word. This is still basically a two-phase call with a single thought pattern for each individual. The first digit represents the series and formation; the second digit represents the pass patterns and the side to which the patterns are run. The first word indicates the backfield pattern and is related to the types of running play. This gives all three parts of the method for calling pass plays dual meanings, simplifies the application of our passing system and helps us to relate with our running plays without having breakdowns.

Now we will examine how we put this system for calling pass plays into multiple application:

1. *The series* are indicated by the first of two digits. We call 10 through 90 series for the shift and the formation. With odd series we get a pro-sets (Figure 11-4). We set the wingback in a wide-flanker set to the calls (patterns). Odd calls are set to the left; even calls are set to the right. With even series we get slot sets (Figure 11-5). We set our wingback in a slot to the left on odd calls and to the right on even calls. The backfield set depends on which series is called.

2. *The patterns* are indicated by the second of two digits. Odd patterns 1 through 9 are to the left, and even patterns 0 through 8 are to the right. Our ends have short primary routes on 0 through 5 patterns and long primary routes on 6 through 9 patterns. Our passing trees shows all our basic patterns for the three basic receivers (Figure 11-6). Since our three basic receivers interchange sets depending on the calls, they must learn all the tree patterns related to their priority of positions. Both ends must learn all three passing trees to both sides. The wingback must learn 1 and 2 priority tree patterns to both sides.

3. *The types of pass plays* are indicated by the first word. We use three basic types of passing plays. These calls are "playaction," "bootleg"

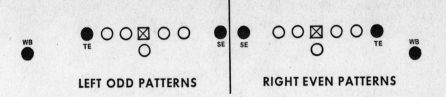

LEFT ODD PATTERNS | **RIGHT EVEN PATTERNS**

FIGURE 11-4: ODD SERIES, WIDE FLANKER PRO-SETS

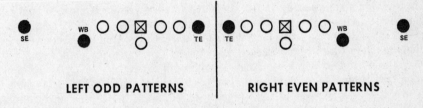

LEFT ODD PATTERNS | **RIGHT EVEN PATTERNS**

FIGURE 11-5: EVEN SERIES, SLOT SETS

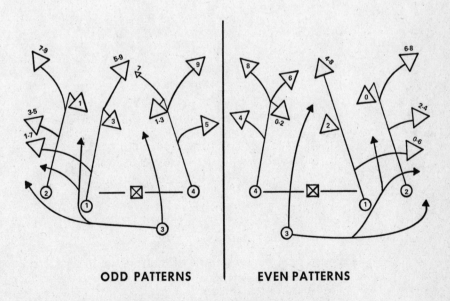

ODD PATTERNS | **EVEN PATTERNS**

FIGURE 11-6: THE PASSING TREES

and "sprintback." They are related to the three basic running techniques. With a *playaction* pass we fake a *power play*. With a *bootleg* pass we fake a *tandem* play. With a *sprintback* pass we run the *sweep* backfield pattern without a fake. We use the same pass blocking rules for all three types of pass plays.

PASS BLOCKING

Pass blocking rules are applied by the interior line. There will be either a defensive down lineman on them or they will be considered uncovered. Any interior lineman who makes contact with a defensive down lineman by moving forward is considered *on* him. If there is no down defensive lineman on an interior lineman, he is uncovered. With even defenses the center is the uncovered interior lineman. Most of the time the guards are uncovered with odd defenses; occasionally the tackles are uncovered. If tackles are uncovered, they block out.

The technique used by an interior lineman when a defensive man is on him is to move forward aggressively,.making contact with his face in the numbers. He must maintain contact with a balanced stutter leg action for five seconds. We apply the stop watch in practice.

The uncovered interior lineman from the call moves forward by taking two short rapid stutter steps, and then pulls to the backside to pick up the first rushing defensive player to the outside of his tackle (Figure 11-7). On even patterns called, the uncovered interior lineman pulls to the left and blocks. On odd patterns called he pulls to the right and blocks. An assigned back out of the backfield blocks to the side the pattern is called. Figure 11-7 shows the uncovered left guard pulling left against an odd defense on an even call and the uncovered center pulling right against an even defense on an odd call.

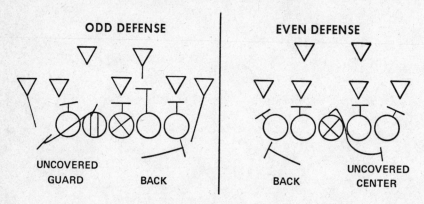

ODD DEFENSE   EVEN DEFENSE

UNCOVERED   UNCOVERED
GUARD   BACK   BACK   CENTER

FIGURE 11-7: PASS BLOCKING RULES

Pass blocking must be aggressive without self-commitment. Daily practice time is required to learn to keep balanced contact and not get one leg too far forward, allowing the defensive man to go around it.

PASS PATTERNS

We have seven basic pass patterns for the four possible receivers we might use. Running them to both sides makes a total of fourteen patterns. Odd patterns are to the left and even patterns are to the right. Remember, the pattern is the second of the digits called and indicates the side to which the pass plays are run.

We will next illustrate the seven basic patterns using seven figures. Each figure will have two parts showing the patterns being run to both the left and right. This is the coordination and application of all three passing trees.

The 0, 1, 2, 3, 4 and 5 patterns have short primary targets with long secondary routes. With the two primary targets we key the defensive man in the short zones. In the secondary patterns we key the deep defensive back's reaction to covering the long or short zones.

Figure 11-8 shows our 1 and 0 pass patterns. The primary patterns are in the short zones. The first priority receiver has the side line pattern. The second priority receiver has the frontside hook area. The fourth priority receiver has the backside hook area. All of the secondary routes are the third priority. They are a result of the quarterback faking the ball with a pumping action. The first priority receiver runs his secondary route straight down the field to complete a staircase pattern. The second priority receiver substitutes a secondary route only if the pass play does not call for a third priority receiver to be released out of the backfield.

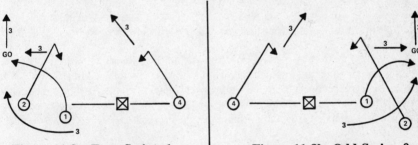

| Figure 11-8a: Even Series, 1 Pattern | Figure 11-8b: Odd Series, 0 Pattern |

FIGURE 11-8: 1 AND 0 PASS PATTERNS

The fourth priority receiver takes his secondary route to Baker. Figure 11-8a shows the 1 pattern run to the left. An even series call gives us a slot set to the left. This gives the wingback first priority and the split end second priority in receiving. Figure 11-8b shows the 0 pattern run to the right. An odd series call gives us a pro-set to the right. This gives the tight end first priority and the wingback set as a wide flanker second priority in their receiving.

Figure 11-9 shows our 3 and 2 pass patterns. The two primary targets trade responsibilities. The first priority receiver has the strongside hook area and the second priority receiver flat (side line) pattern. The fourth priority receiver has

Figure 11-9a: Odd Series, 3
Pattern

Figure 11-9b: Even Series, 2
Pattern

FIGURE 11-9: 3 AND 2 PASS PATTERNS

the backside hook area. Again, all the secondary routes are third in priority after the quarterback has made his pumping motion. The first priority receiver will run his secondary route to the cleared out flat if the third priority receiver has not been released out of the backfield. The second priority receiver completes a staircase pattern on his secondary route. The fourth priority receiver takes his secondary route to Baker. Figure 11-9a shows the 3 pattern run to the left. An odd series call gives us a pro-set to the left. This gives the tight end first priority and the wide flanker second priority in their receiving. Figure 11-9b shows the 2 pattern being run to the right. An even series call gives us a slot set to the right. This gives the wingback first priority and the split end second priority in their receiving.

Figure 11-10 shows our 4 and 5 pass patterns. Basically both outside receivers run sideline patterns, and our inside receiver splits the short middle. They go to their respective three-deep zones on their secondary routes. The first priority receiver runs over the short middle. The second priority receiver runs the sideline pattern to the frontside of the call. The third priority receiver is out of the

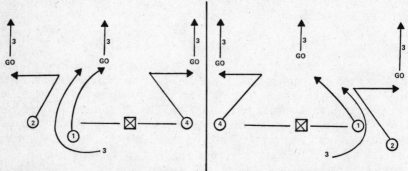

Figure 11-10a: Even Series, 5
Pattern

Figure 11-10b: Odd Series, 4
Pattern

FIGURE 11-10: 4 AND 5 PASS PATTERNS

backfield and splits the primary targets to the frontside. The fourth priority receiver runs the backside flat pattern. They all four have secondary routes after the quarterback's pumping motion. The second and fourth priority receiver complete their staircase patterns. The first priority receiver goes to Baker on his secondary route, and the third priority receiver goes to the middle area that has been left cleared out. Figure 11-10a shows the 5 pattern run to the left. An even series call gives us a slot set to the left. This gives the wingback first priority and the split end secondary priority in their receiving. Figure 11-10b shows the 4 pattern run to the right. An odd series gives us a pro-set to the right. This gives the tight end first priority and the wide flanker secondary priority in their receiving.

The following two pass patterns are supplements of the 1 and 0 patterns. They are an influence of the "give and go" and "pick and roll" basketball plays. These maneuvers are even more effective in getting a man open as a pass receiver in football than they are on the hard wood. This is because neither of the two men involved in the maneuvers have the ball, and it is naturally predetermined. Only the two primary targets vary from the 1 and 0 patterns. The primary receivers will run the "drag and go" and the "go and drag" patterns. The outgrowth of these two patterns was influenced by the fact that the two primary receivers run to the fifth defensive man before making their cuts on all of the short patterns. The go man will always make the pick for the drag man on both patterns. The go man breaks first. The two primary receivers will alternate these "Go" and "Drag" responsibilities from one pattern to the next as called.

Figure 11-11 shows and 1 and 0 "drag and go" pass patterns. The two primary targets have no secondary routes. The first priority receiver has the "drag" call and the second priority receiver has the "go" call. Both receivers set screens on the fifth defensive man. When the second priority receiver breaks on his "go" pattern, the first priority receiver reverses his route back across the short middle. The third priority receiver flares in behind the cleared out short zone. The fourth priority runs his backside hook pattern and then takes his secondary route to Baker zone. Figure 11-11a shows the 1 "drag and go" patterns run to the left. An even series call gives us a slot set left. This gives the wingback the drag pattern, and the split end the go pattern. Figure 11-11b shows

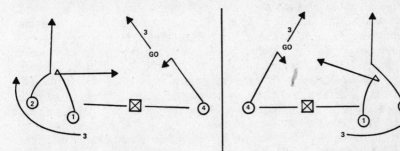

Figure 11-11a: Even Series, 1
Pattern

Figure 11-11b: Even Series, 0
Pattern

FIGURE 11-11: DRAG AND GO PASS PATTERNS

the 0 "drag and go" patterns run to the right. An even series call gives us a slot set right. Again the wingback has the drag pattern and the split end has the go pattern. The drag always has priority over the go pattern.

Figure 11-12 shows the 1 and 0 "go and drag" pass patterns. The two primary targets switch assignments. The first priority receiver has the "go" call and the second priority receiver has the "drag" call. Both receivers pick the fifth defensive man. When the first priority receiver breaks on his go pattern, the second priority cuts off his screen over the short middle. The third priority receiver flares to the cleared out short zone. The fourth priority receiver runs his backside hook pattern and then takes his secondary route to Baker. Figure 11-11a shows the 1 "go and drag" patterns run to the left. An even series call gives us a slot set to the left. This gives the wingback the "go" pattern and the split end the "drag" pattern. Figure 11-11b shows the 0 "go and drag" patterns run to the right. An odd series call gives us a pro-set to the right. This gives the tight end the "go" pattern and the wide flanker the "drag" pattern.

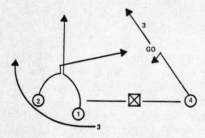 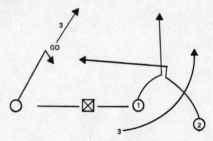

Figure 11-12a: Even Series, 1   **Figure 11-12b: Odd Series, 0**
Pattern   **Pattern**

FIGURE 11-12: GO AND DRAG PASS PATTERNS

The 6, 7, 8 and 9 patterns are our long patterns. The two ends run the deep patterns as secondary targets; the backs run the short patterns as primary targets.

Figure 11-13 shows the 7 and 6 pass patterns. The first priority receiver runs a sideline pattern to the short zone. He cuts off the back of the second priority receiver into the flat. The second priority receiver cuts off the 5th defensive man and sprints to the outside shoulder. The third priority receiver cuts back behind the primary target toward hook area. The fourth priority receiver sprints to Baker zone. Figure 11-13a shows the 7 pattern run to the left. The odd series gives us a pro-set to the left. The tight end is the first priority receiver to Easy zone, and the wide flanker is the second priority receiver to Able zone. The split end is the backside end who sprints to Baker zone. Figure 11-13b shows the 6 pattern run to the right. The even series gives us a slot set to the right. The wingback is the first priority receiver to Dog zone, and the split end is the second priority receiver to Charlie zone. The tight end is the backside end to Baker zone.

Figure 11-14 shows the 9 and 8 pass patterns. The third and fourth priority receivers are set wide and run their patterns to the deep outside zones looking

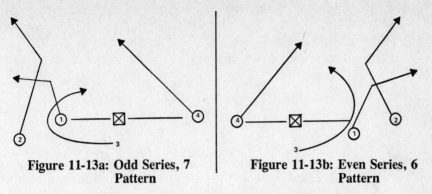

Figure 11-13a: Odd Series, 7 Pattern

Figure 11-13b: Even Series, 6 Pattern

FIGURE 11-13: 7 AND 6 PASS PATTERNS

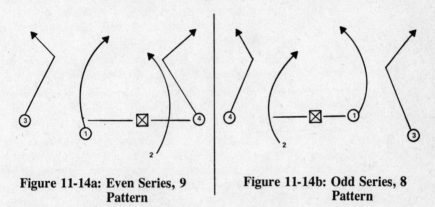

Figure 11-14a: Even Series, 9 Pattern

Figure 11-14b: Odd Series, 8 Pattern

FIGURE 11-14: 9 AND 8 PASS PATTERNS

over their outside shoulders. This isolates the defensive safety in Baker zone. Our two primary receivers will two on one the safety. The first priority receiver's route to Baker zone is through the frontside, and the second priority receiver's route to Baker is through the backside. Figure 11-14a shows the 9 pattern run to the left. The even series gives us a slot set to the left. The wingback is the first priority receiver to Baker zone along with the second priority receiver out of the backfield. The split end is the third priority receiver to Able zone, and the tight end is the fourth priority receiver to Charlie zone. Figure 11-14b shows the 8 pattern run to the right. An odd series call gives us a pro-set to the right. The tight end is the first priority receiver to Baker zone along with the second priority receiver out of the backfield. The wide flanker is the third priority receiver to Charlie zone, and the split end is the fourth priority receiver to Able zone.

This gives us a total of fourteen pass patterns. We can apply any one of these patterns we might need with all of our backfield actions and formations.

This results in a very multiple passing system. Before we put these patterns into multiple application, we need to establish a method for recognizing defensive secondary coverage and how to run the patterns against them.

RECOGNIZING DEFENSIVE SECONDARY COVERAGE

There are two general kinds of defensive pass coverages: zones and man-to-man. There are also combinations of the two. Let us examine their characteristics so we can learn to recognize them and their weaknesses so we can take advantage of them.

1. *Zone pass defense* have men responsible for assigned areas and the coverage of any pass receiver who enters them. These areas are usually three deep zones and range from two to four short zones. It is the best coverage against the bomb and usually produces the highest percentage of interceptions. Its weakness is that the zones may be split by the fast deployment of receivers between the zones. This forces the defensive players to make choices prior to coverage. It is difficult to maintain zone coverage against double wing or slot formations.

2. *Man-to-man pass defense* is the simplest to understand and learn, and the most fundamentally and tactically sound. The biggest difficulty with it is in matching abilities in personnel or maintaining a tactical balance in speed. If their receivers are bigger and faster than your pass defenders, then you will be forced to zone coverage.

Straight zone or man-to-man coverages are easy to recognize and overcome. It is the combinations of both kinds of coverage that can confuse our passers. A three-deep secondary can be the most confusing. With a two-deep secondary with outside cornerbacks, you can expect outside zone rotation; with a four-deep secondary, you can anticipate inside zone rotation. With a three-deep secondary, you have to look for everything. Three deep can be in man-to-man, zone or combination coverage. The halfbacks can cover man to man, while the safety is involved with inside rotating zone coverage. A three-deep man-to-man coverage is usually combined with zone linebacker coverage. They can be in the form of monsters or rovers. No matter how good a quarterback is at reading the defense, his biggest shock has to be when he throws to a receiver wide open in Baker and has it intercepted. There are many coaches who will not accept that it is sound for a backside linebacker to cover middle deep. A well-trained backside linebacker can sometimes have a better shot at catching the ball than your frontside receiver. This is one of several reasons why zone coverages get more interceptions, and why we will concentrate on recognizing and reacting against three-deep defensive coverage.

Figure 11-15 shows our method of recognizing three-deep defensive coverage. Our quarterback reads the safety before the snap and keys the fifth man after the snap. If the safety is in Baker, it is considered zone coverage (Figure 11-15a). If the safety is in Able or Charlie, he is playing either our tight end or wingback man-to-man (Figure 11-15b). Against zone coverages our receivers split the difference between the two defensive players in their target areas (Figure 11-15a). Against man-to-man coverage our receivers run directly toward their defensive men and make their cuts off him (Figure 11-15b). Figure 11-15 shows

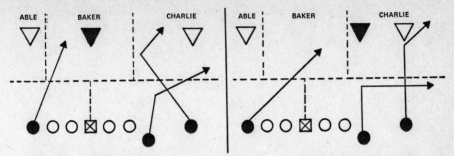

Figure 11-15a: Zone Coverage   **Figure 11-15b: Man-to-Man Coverage**

FIGURE 11-15: RECOGNITION OF DEFENSE COVERAGE

the variation of our receivers' initial routes against both zone (Figure 11-15a) and man-to-man (Figure 11-15b) coverage in running the same pattern.

Because of our specialized two platoon program we have 25 minutes per practice for our offensive backs and receivers to work against our defensive backs. Our pass defense uses a combination of man-to-man and zone coverage with three deep and two cornerbacks. We both learn from each other and it becomes very competitive. Our passers and receivers learn to recognize and execute within two steps after the snap. This results in game situations being much easier than application in practice.

This completes our basic elements for our multiple passing system. We have established eight sets from series calls and fourteen patterns we can run. We have three types of pass plays. Multiply these elements, and we can total a possible 336 pass plays we can call. This is not practical: next we need a method to put these three elements together and at the same time limit them in application. The following chapter deals with the multiple application of our passing system.

CHAPTER 12

Coordinating the Multiple Application of the Power "I" Passing Game

As with our running game, there is need for controls with the multiple application of our passing attack. There are several reasons for this. Our pass plays and formations should be related to our running attack. At the same time, we want to limit our pass calls to only using what we need. Too much offense with unnecessary calls can cause breakdowns that could hurt us. There are times when a pass play should start as if it is going to be a running play. There are other situations when there is no reason for a fake before the pass. Next we will coordinate the calls for controlling our multiple application.

COORDINATING THE CALLS FOR MULTIPLE APPLICATION

During the successful running of our power option plays we need to mix the fake pass in with the sequence. The quarterback lead steps with a fake ride to the fullback before passing. It is run out of a fullhouse "I" backfield set to the tight side of a balanced line on a 30 series call and the split side of a balanced line on a 40 series call. We call "playaction" to fake a power. We only use four short patterns with playaction passes: the 0 and 2 patterns to the right and the 1 and 3 patterns to the left (Figure 12-1—Coordination categories).

We fake tandem and isolation running plays and then the bootleg pass from the calls. The pass call is "bootleg," and is run from a fullhouse "I" backfield set. We fake the fullback "iso" on 30 and 40 series calls and tailback tandems on 50 and 60 series calls. With bootleg passes we only make an occasional even

170

PASS PLAYS		CALLS		
BACKFIELD ACTIONS	FORMATIONS	SERIES	PATTERNS	TYPES
1. FAKE FULLBACK POWERS	FULL HOUSE	30-40	0-1-2-3	PLAYACTION
2. FAKE FULLBACK ISOS	FULL HOUSE	30-40	4-5	BOOT LEG
3. FAKE TAILBACK TANDEMS	FULL HOUSE	50-60	4-5	BOOT LEG
4. FRONTSIDE	PRO SETS	10-50	ALL OF THEM	SPRINT BACK
5. FRONTSIDE	SLOT SETS	20-60	ALL OF THEM	SPRINT BACK
6. BACKSIDE	SLOT SETS	90	ALL OF THEM	SPRINT BACK

FIGURE 12-1: CO-ORDINATING THE PASSING SYSTEM

series call. Most of the time it is an odd series call. We only use 5 or 4 patterns (Figure 12-1—Coordination categories).

Our *sprintback* passes are run without a fake. This releases a fourth receiver out of the backfield. He has third priority as a primary receiver and first priority as a secondary receiver. We use all of our patterns with all sprintback calls. These patterns are concentrated within multiple formations. With the 10 and 50 series calls we get frontside pro-sets. The 10 series gives us a wide flanker "T" backfield set, and the 50 series gives us a wide flanker "I" backfield set. With the 20 and 60 series calls, we get frontside slot sets. The 20 series gives us slot "T" backfield sets, and the 60 series gives us slot "I" backfield sets. The 90 sprintback series is very unique. We run all the patterns to the backside of a slot "T" set. The receiver out of the backfield goes to the call which is away from the patterns (Figure 12-1—Coordination categories).

This method for coordination will assure us to use the correct patterns with the related backfield actions and sets. Next we will put our passing system into proper multiple application.

PLAYACTION PASSES

In running playaction passes to the tight side of a balanced line we use a 30 series call (Figure 12-2). We will show all four patterns used against a variation of defensive situations.

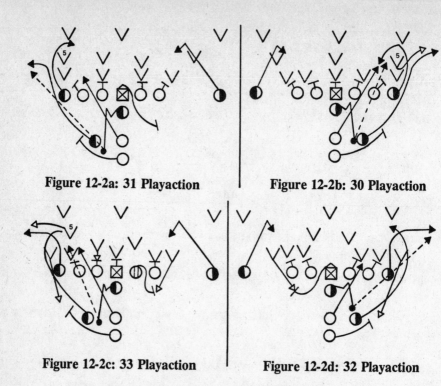

Figure 12-2a: 31 Playaction   **Figure 12-2b: 30 Playaction**

Figure 12-2c: 33 Playaction   **Figure 12-2d: 32 Playaction**

FIGURE 12-2: 30 SERIES, PLAYACTION PASSES

Figure 12-2a shows a 31 playaction pass being run against a 44 stack defense. There is a fullhouse power "I" backfield set to the left tight side. The center pulls to protect the backside. The tailback blocks to the frontside. The quarterback fakes a 33 power and keys their cornerback (fifth man). The cornerback covers the tight end. The wingback runs his Easy pattern from his halfback set and receives the ball on his cut. He is the first priority receiver.

Figure 12-2b shows a 30 play action pass being run against an eagle 53 defense. There is a fullhouse power "I" backfield set to the right tight side. There is no uncovered interior lineman to pull to the backside. The tailback blocks to the right. The quarterback fakes a 32 power and keys the cornerback who covers his first priority receiver in Dog. He passes to his second priority receiver who is the tight end in the hook area.

Figure 12-2c shows a 33 play action pass being run against a 52 monster defense. There is a fullhouse "I" backfield set to the left tight side. The uncovered right guard pulls to protect the right backside. The tailback blocks to the left. The quarterback fakes a 33 power to the fullback. The cornerback covers the tight end in Easy leaving the wingback open in the hook area. He is the primary target. Notice that the backside split end might be open: his call must be predetermined.

Figure 12-2d shows a 32 play action pass being run against a split 62

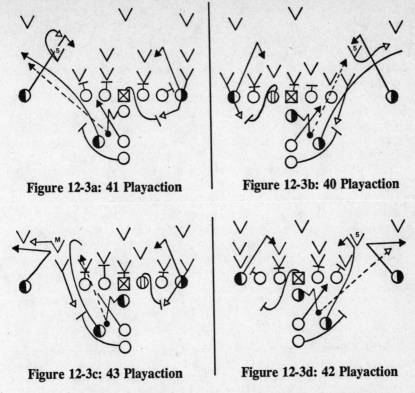

Figure 12-3a: 41 Playaction | Figure 12-3b: 40 Playaction

Figure 12-3c: 43 Playaction | Figure 12-3d: 42 Playaction

FIGURE 12-3: 40 SERIES, PLAYACTION PASSES

defense. There is a fullhouse "I" backfield set to the right. The uncovered center pulls left and protects the backside. The tailback blocks right. The quarterback fakes a 32 power to the fullback and passes to the open tight end in Dog on his cut.

In running playaction passes to the splitside of a balanced line, we use a 40 series call (Figure 12-3). Again we use the same four short patterns against a variety of defenses.

Figure 12-3a shows a 41 play action pass being run against a 44 stack defense. There is a fullhouse "I" backfield set to the left split side. The uncovered center pulls right to protect the backside. The tailback blocks to the left. The quarterback fakes a 43 power to the fullback before passing to his first priority receiver who is open in Easy. The wingback was open because their cornerback covered our split end in the hook area.

Figure 12-3b shows a 40 play action pass being run against a 52 monster defense. There is a fullhouse "I" backfield set to the right split side. The uncovered left guard pulls back and protects the left side. The tailback blocks to the right. The quarterback fakes a 42 power to the fullback before passing to the split end who was the second priority target in the hook area. The monster covered the first priority wingback Dog zone.

Figure 12-3c shows a 43 play action pass being run against a 52 monster defense. There is a fullhouse "I" backfield set to the left split side. The uncovered right guard pulls back to the right to protect the backside. The tailback blocks to the left. The quarterback fakes a 43 power to the fullback before passing to his first priority wingback in the hook area. He was open because the linebacker covered the second priority split end in Easy.

Figure 12-3d shows a 42 playaction pass being run against a 44 stack defense. There is a fullhouse "I" backfield set to the right split side. The uncovered center pulls to the left to protect the backside. The tailback blocks to the right. The quarterback fakes a 42 power to the fullback before he passes to his second priority split end who is open in Dog. This is because the first priority wingback was covered by the cornerback in the hook area.

These are all the play action passes that are necessary to complement our power option running sequence. Take into consideration that we mix in tandem and isolation running plays in short yardage situations. Everytime we run our tandems or isolations our quarterback bootlegs from the call checking the backside for a possible pass call. If he finds the backside open, he will call a bootleg pass. Only one basic pattern to both sides will be used with our bootleg passes. The quarterback has the option to pass or run to the backside after he has faked a tandem or isolation.

BOOTLEG PASSES

On bootleg passes the quarterback reverse pivots to the call before his fake. This gives the needed delay for the defensive reaction. After faking either a fullback isolation or a tailback tandem, he bootlegs away from the call. We use the 30 and 40 series for fullback "iso" calls, and the 50 and 60 series for tailback tandem calls. We only use 4 and 5 pass patterns. The uncovered interior lineman who pulls to block the backside uses his sweep technique after his two-count delay.

In running bootleg passes that follow a fullback "iso" fake to the tight side of a balanced line, we use a 30 series call (Figure 12-4).

Figure 12-4a shows a 35 bootleg pass being run against a 44 stack defense. There is a fullhouse power "I" backfield set to the left tight side. The quarterback reverse pivots before faking a 35 isolation. The tailback blocks to the call. The uncovered center pulls to the right and blocks for the quarterback, who bootlegs from the call. Their backside cornerback covers our split end in his sideline pattern at Dog. This open leaves the wingback whose route was from Easy to Dog after the area had been cleared out.

Figure 12-4b shows a 34 bootleg pass being run against a 52 monster defense. Since the monster is set to the wingback side, the play will end up being run from the monster. There is a fullhouse power "I" backfield set to the right tight side. The quarterback reverse pivots before faking a 34 isolation. The tailback blocks to the right. The uncovered left guard pulls to the left and blocks for the quarterback's bootleg. Since the monster is set to the right, our split end is left open in the left Easy zone.

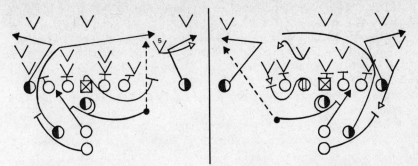

Figure 12-4a: 35 Bootleg   Figure 12-4b: 34 Bootleg

FIGURE 12-4: 30 SERIES, BOOTLEG PASSES

In running bootleg passes that follow a fullback "iso" fake to the split side of a balanced line, we use a 40 series call (Figure 12-5).

Figure 12-5a shows a 45 bootleg pass being run against a 52 monster defense. There is a fullhouse power "I" backfield set to the left split side. The quarterback reverse pivots before faking a 45 "iso." The tailback blocks to the left. The uncovered right guard pulls to the right and blocks for the quarterback who bootlegs from the call. Since the monster is set to the left, our tight end is left open in the right Dog zone.

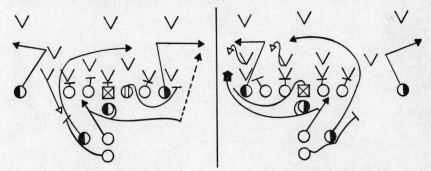

Figure 12-5a: 45 Bootleg   Figure 12-5b: 44 Bootleg

FIGURE 12-5: 40 SERIES, BOOTLEG PASSES

Figure 12-5b shows a 44 bootleg pass being run against a 44 stack defense. There is a fullhouse power "I" backfield set to the right split side. The quarterback reverse pivots before faking a 44 "iso." The tailback blocks to the right. The uncovered center pulls to the left and blocks for the quarterback who bootlegs from the call. Since both receivers are covered, the quarterback keeps the ball and runs.

In running bootleg passes that follow a tailback tandem fake to the tight side of a balanced line, we use a 50 series call (Figure 12-6).

Figure 12-6a shows a 55 bootleg pass being run against a split 62 defense. There is a fullhouse power ''I'' backfield set to the left tight side of a balanced line. The quarterback reverse pivots before faking a 53 tandem to the tailback. the fullback blocks to the left. The uncovered center pulls to the right and blocks for the quarterback who bootlegs from the call. The split end is open in the right Dog zone.

Figure 12-6b shows a 54 bootleg pass being run against an eagle 53 defense. There is a fullhouse power ''I'' backfield set to the right tight side of a balanced

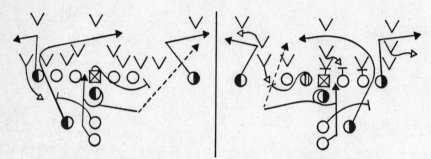

Figure 12-6a: 55 Bootleg   **Figure 12-6b: 54 Bootleg**

FIGURE 12-6: 50 SERIES, BOOTLEG PASSES

line. The quarterback reverse pivots before faking a 52 tandem to the tailback. The fullback blocks to the right. The uncovered left guard pulls to the left and blocks for the quarterback who pulls from the call. Since the tailback's fake freezes the middle linebacker and the cornerback covers the split end in Easy, it leaves the wingback open in the cleared out area.

In running bootleg passes that follow a tailback tandem fake to the split side of a balanced line, we use a 60 series call (Figure 12-7).

Figure 12-7a shows a 65 bootleg pass being run against a pro-43 defense. There is a fullhouse power ''I'' backfield set to the left split side of a balanced line. The quarterback reverse pivots before faking a 61 tandem to the tailback. The fullback blocks to the left. The uncovered center pulls to the right and blocks for the quarterback who bootlegs from the call. Since both of the receivers are covered in Dog zone, the quarterback runs with the ball.

Figure 12-7b shows a 64 bootleg pass being run against a 52 monster defense. The monster is set to our wingback's side. The quarterback reverse pivots before faking a 60 tandem to the tailback. The fullback blocks to the right.The uncovered left guard pulls to the left and blocks for the quarterback who bootlegs from the call. Since the monster is set to our right it will leave our tight end open in Easy zone.

This completes the basic passing attack that complements our basic running game. We fake our power option sequences with play action passes and fake our

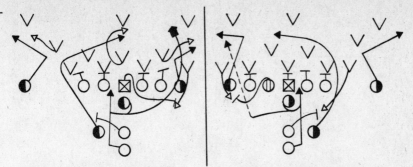

Figure 12-7a: 65 Bootleg   Figure 12-7b: 64 Bootleg

FIGURE 12-7: 60 SERIES, BOOTLEG PASSES

tandem and isolation plays with bootleg passes. All of these passes have a fake with three possible receivers. The majority of our passes are sprintbacks. With sprintback passes there are no fakes. This releases a fourth receiver into our patterns. With these patterns we concentrate on our formations and try to take advantage of their defensive sets. We use pro-sets and slot sets with all of our patterns in three ways:

First, with a pro-set we split our wingback to a wide flanker set. Our primary targets are the tight end with first priority and our wingback with second priority. We send the fourth receiver into the primary target areas after they have been cleared out.

Second, we set our wingback in a tight slot with first priority and the split end having second priority as primary targets. Again we send the fourth receiver into the primary target area after it has been cleared out.

Third, we set our wingback in a wide slot and run all of our patterns to the backside of our set. We release our fourth receiver to the short frontside zones away from the basic patterns.

Now we will show the multiple application of the sprintback passing attack. This will require a shift from the full house "I" backfield set.

PASSING FROM THE PRO-SET

We get our pro-sets by making an odd series sprintback call. A 10 series call gives us a floater "T" backfield set, and a 50 series call gives us a wide flanker "I" set. In both cases the wingback sets to the calls as a wide flanker. He is the second priority receiver. The tight end is the first priority receiver. The split end is set from the call as a fourth priority receiver. The tailback released as a fourth receiver from the backfield has third priority as a primary receiver and first priority as a secondary receiver.

Figure 12-8 shows 11 and 10 sprintback passes. They are the same plays

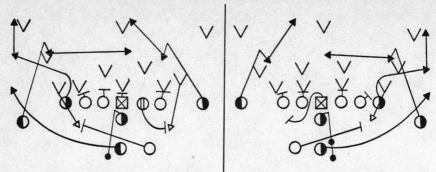

Figure 12-8a: 11 Sprintback   Figure 12-8b: 10 Sprintback

FIGURE 12-8: 10 SERIES, PRO-SET PASSES

except that one is run to the left against an odd defense and the other is run to the right against an even defense:

Figure 12-8a shows an 11 sprintback pass being run against a 52 monster defense. There is a wide flanker "T" backfield set to the left tight side with the split end set from the call. The uncovered right guard pulls to protect the right backside. The fullback blocks to the left front side from his right half set. The quarterback sprints straight back, keying the monster in Easy zone. The primary targets are the tight end with first priority in the flat and the wingback with second priority in the hook area. The tight end runs his secondary route which results in a staircase pattern. The tailback fills the cleared out zone. The quarterback's passing options are all focused in Easy zone.

Figure 12-8b shows a 10 sprintback pass being run against a 44 stack defense. There is a wide flanker "T" backfield set to the right tight side with the split end set to the left. The uncovered center pulls to protect the left backside. The fullback blocks to the right from his left half set. The quarterback sprints back keying the primary targets and secondary routes in and out of Dog zone.

Figure 12-9 shows 11 and 10 (drag and go) sprintback passes. They are both the same plays with one being run to the left against an even defense and the other being run to the right against an odd defense:

Figure 12-9a shows an 11 drag and go sprintback pass being run against a pro 43 defense. There is a wide flanker "T" backfield set to the left tight side with the split end set to the right. The uncovered center pulls right to protect the backside. The fullback blocks to the left from his right half set. The quarterback sprints back keying the cornerback in Easy zone. The tight end has the drag pattern back toward the Dog zone, and wingback has the go pattern to Able zone. The tailback flares to the cleared out Easy zone.

Figure 12-9b shows a 10 drag and go sprintback pass being run against a 52 monster defense. There is a wide flanker "T" backfield set to the right tight side with the split end set to the left. The uncovered left guard pulls left to protect the backside. The fullback blocks to the right from his left half set. The quarterback sprints back keying the monster in Dog zone. The tight end has the drag pattern

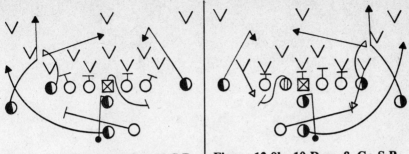

Figure 12-9a: Drag & Go, 11 S.B. | **Figure 12-9b: 10 Drag & Go S.B.**

FIGURE 12-9: 10 SERIES, PRO-SET PASSES

back toward Easy zone, and the wingback has the go pattern to Charlie zone. The tailback flares to the cleared out Dog zone.

Figure 12-10 shows 11 and 10 (go and drag) sprintback passes. They are both the same play with one being run to the left against an even defense and the other being run to the right against an odd defense.

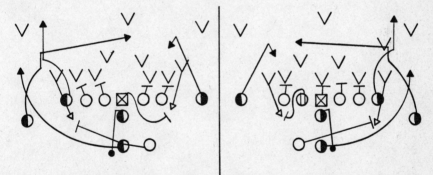

Figure 12-10a: 11 Go & Drag S.B. | **Figure 12-10b: 10 Go & Drag S.B.**

FIGURE 12-10: 10 SERIES, PRO-SET PASSES

Figure 12-10a shows an 11 go and drag sprintback pass being run against a split 62 defense. There is a wide flanker "T" backfield set to the left tight side with the split end set to the right. The uncovered center pulls to the right to protect the backside. The fullback blocks to the left from his right half set. The quarterback sprints back with his focus on Easy zone. The tight end has the go pattern to Able zone, and the wingback has the drag pattern toward Dog zone. The tailback flares to the cleared out Easy zone.

Figure 12-10b shows a 10 go and drag sprintback pass being run against a 52 monster defense. There is a wide flanker "T" backfield set to the right tight side with the split end set to the left. The uncovered left guard pulls to the left to protect the backside. The fullback blocks to the right from his left half set. The quarterback sprints back with his focus on Dog zone. The tight end has the go pattern to Charlie zone, and the wingback has the drag pattern toward Easy zone. The tailback flares to the cleared out Dog zone.

Figure 12-11 shows 13 and 12 sprintback passes. They are both the same play with one being run to the left against an odd defense and the other being run to the right against an even defense.

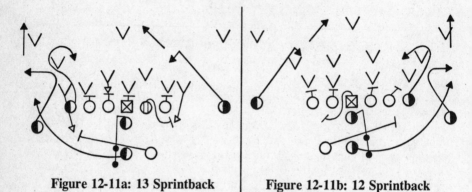

Figure 12-11a: 13 Sprintback   **Figure 12-11b: 12 Sprintback**

FIGURE 12-11: 10 SERIES, PRO-SET PASSES

Figure 12-11a shows a 13 sprintback pass being run against a 52 monster defense. There is a wide flanker "T" backfield set to the left tight side with the split end set to the right. The uncovered right guard pulls right to protect the backside. The fullback blocks to the left from his right half set. The quarterback sprints back keying the monster in Easy zone. The primary targets are the wingback with first priority in Easy zone and the tight end with second priority in the hook area. The wingback runs his secondary route to Able zone which results in a staircase pattern. The tailback flares to the cleared out Easy zone.

Figure 12-11b shows a 12 sprintback pass being run against a 44 stack defense. There is a wide flanker "T" backfield set to the right tight side with the split end set to the left. The uncovered center pulls to the left to protect the backside. The fullback blocks to the right from his left half set. The quarterback sprints back keying the right corner back in Dog zone. The primary targets are the wingback with first priority in Dog and the tight end with second priority in the hook area. The wingback runs his secondary route to Charlie zone which results in a staircase pattern. The tailback flares to the cleared out Dog zone.

Figure 12-12 shows 15 and 14 sprintback passes. They are both the same play with one being run to the left against an even defense and the other being run to the right against an odd defense.

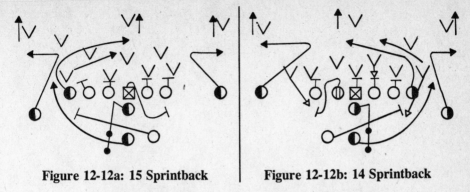

Figure 12-12a: 15 Sprintback | **Figure 12-12b: 14 Sprintback**

FIGURE 12-12: 10 SERIES, PRO-SET PASSES

Figure 12-12a shows a 15 sprintback pass being run against a pro-43 defense. The pro-set is left. The uncovered center pulls to the right to protect the backside. The fullback blocks to the left from his right half set. The quarterback sprints back keying the left corner back in Easy zone. The tight end and wingback both run at the cornerback before they cut on their primary routes. The tailback splits to the hook area. Both ends and the wingback go to their three-deep zones on secondary routes. The tailback cuts over the short middle on his secondary route.

Figure 12-12b shows a 14 sprintback pass being run against a 52 monster defense. The pro-set is right. The uncovered left guard pulls to the left to protect the backside. The fullback blocks to the right from his left half set. The quarterback sprints back, keying the monster in Dog zone. The wingback and tight end both run at the monster before they make their cuts on their primary routes. The tailback splits the monster's area. Both ends and the wingback go to their three-deep zones on secondary routes. The tailback cuts over the short middle on his secondary route.

Figure 12-13 shows 17 and 16 sprintback passes. They are both the same play with one being run to the left against an odd defense and the other being run to the right against an even defense.

Figure 12-13a shows a 17 sprintback pass being run against a 52 monster defense. The pro-set is to the left. The uncovered right guard pulls to the right to protect the backside. The fullback blocks to his left from his right half set. The quarterback sprints back with his focus on Easy zone. The wingback makes his cut off the monster for Able zone. The tight end is the primary target in Easy. If the monster covers him, the quarterback will hit the tailback cutting back over the hook area toward Baker.

Figure 12-13b shows a 16 sprintback pass being run against a 44 stack defense. The pro-set is to the right. The uncovered center pulls to the left to protect the backside. The fullback blocks to his right from his left half set. The quarterback sprints back with his focus on Dog zone. The wingback makes his

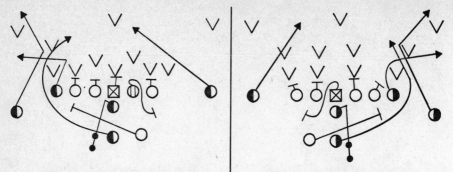

Figure 12-13a: 17 Sprintback   **Figure 12-13b: 16 Sprintback**

FIGURE 12-13: 10 SERIES, PRO-SET PASSES

cut off of the cornerback for Charlie zone. The tight end is the primary target in Dog. The tailback cuts back over the hook area toward Baker.

Figure 12-14 shows 19 and 18 sprintback passes. They are only called in desperate situations against prevent defenses. When we need the bomb against three-deep zone coverage, the situation is critical but not impossible. We send four receivers long against three-deep coverage. The two wide receivers isolate at Able and Charlie. The two inside receivers' routes are to Baker so they can two-on-one the safety. These plays are both the same with one being run to the left against an even defense and the other being run to the right against an odd defense.

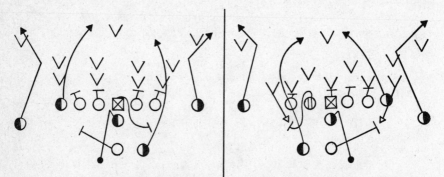

Figure 12-14a: 19 Sprintback   **Figure 12-14b: 18 Sprintback**

FIGURE 12-14: 10 SERIES, PRO-SET PASSES

Figure 12-14a shows a 19 sprintback pass being run against a 44 stack defense. The pro-set is to the left. The uncovered center pulls to the right to protect the backside. The fullback and tailback have switched assignments. The tailback blocks to the left from his fullback set. The wingback's route is to outside Able and the split end goes to outside Charlie. The tight end splits Able and Baker, and the fullback splits Baker and Charlie. The quarterback sprints back and keys the safety. He tries to hit the receiver in Baker whom the safety has not covered.

Figure 12-14b shows an 18 sprintback pass being run against a 52 monster defense. The pro-set is to the right. The uncovered left guard pulls to the left and protects the backside. The fullback and tailback have switched assignments. The tailback blocks to the right from his fullback set. The wingback's pattern is to outside Charlie, and the split end's pattern is to outside Able. The tight end splits Baker and Charlie, and the fullback splits Able and Baker. The quarterback sprints back and keys the safety. He tries to hit the receiver in Baker that the safety has not covered.

PASSING FROM THE SLOT

We prefer passing from the slot rather than the pro-set. We get our slots by making an even sprintback series call. A 20 series call gives us a slot "T" backfield set; a 60 series call gives us a slot "I" backfield set. In both cases the wingback sets in a tight slot to the inside of the split end. They are both set to the call, and the tight end is set from the call. The wingback is the first priority receiver, the split end is the second priority receiver and the tight end has fourth priority. The tailback released as a fourth receiver from the backfield has third priority as a primary receiver and first priority as a secondary receiver.

Figure 12-15 shows 21 and 20 sprintback passes. These plays are both the same with one being run to the left against an odd defense and the other being run to the right against an even defense.

Figure 12-15a shows a 21 sprintback pass being run against an eagle 53 defense. The slot is set to the left. The uncovered right guard pulls to the right and protects the backside, and the fullback blocks left from a right half set. The wingback has first priority in Easy; the split end has second priority in the hook area. The tailback flares to Easy after the primary targets have cleared out on their secondary routes.

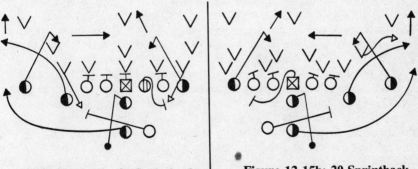

Figure 12-15a: 21 Sprintback   Figure 12-15b: 20 Sprintback

FIGURE 12-15: 20 SERIES, SLOT SET PASSES

Figure 12-15b shows a 20 sprintback pass being run against a split 44 defense. The slot is set to the right. The uncovered center pulls to the left and protects the backside and the fullback blocks right from a left half set. The wingback has first priority in Dog with the split end being open in the hook area. The tailback flares to Dog after the primary targets have left on their secondary routes.

Figure 12-16 shows 21 and 20 (drag and go) sprintback passes. These plays are both the same with one being run to the left against an odd defense and the other being run to the right against an even defense.

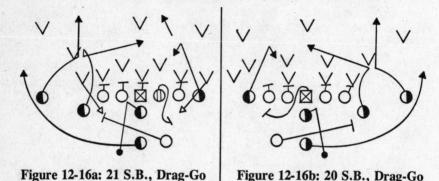

Figure 12-16a: 21 S.B., Drag-Go | **Figure 12-16b: 20 S.B., Drag-Go**

FIGURE 12-16: 20 SERIES, SLOT SET PASSES

Figure 12-16a shows a 21 drag and go sprintback pass being run against a 52 monster defense. The slot is set to the left. The uncovered right guard pulls to the right and protects the backside, and the fullback blocks to the left from his right half set. The quarterback sprints back and keys the monster in Easy zone. The wingback has the drag pattern back across the middle, and the split end has the go pattern to Able zone. The tailback flares to Easy.

Figure 12-16b shows a 20 drag and go sprintback pass being run against a 44 stack defense. The slot is set to the right. The uncovered center pulls to the left to protect the backside, and the fullback blocks to the right from his left half set. The quarterback sprints back and keys the cornerback in Dog. The wingback has the drag pattern back across the middle, and the split end has the go pattern to Charlie. The tailback flares to Dog.

Figure 12-17 shows 21 and 20 (go and drag) sprintback passes. These plays are both the same with one being run to the left against an even defense and the other being run to the right against an odd defense.

Figure 12-17a shows a 21 go and drag pass being run against a stack 44 defense. The slot set is to the left. The uncovered center pulls to the right to protect the backside, and the fullback blocks to the left from his right half set. The quarterback keys the cornerback in Easy. The wingback has the go pattern to Able; the split end has the drag pattern behind his pick. The tailback flares to Easy.

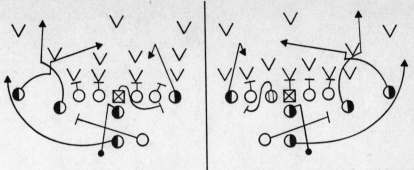

Figure 12-17a: 21 S.B., Go-Drag | **Figure 12-17b: 20 S.B., Go-Drag**

FIGURE 12-17: 20 SERIES, SLOT SET PASSES

Figure 12-17b shows a 20 go and drag pass being run against a 52 monster defense. The slot set is to the right. The uncovered left guard pulls to the left and protects the backside; the fullback blocks right from his left half set. The quarterback keys in the monster in Dog. The wingback has the go pattern to Charlie and the split end has the drag pattern behind his pick. The tailback flares to Dog.

Figure 12-18 shows 23 and 22 sprintback passes. They are both the same plays with one being run to the left against an odd defense and the other being run to the right against an even defense.

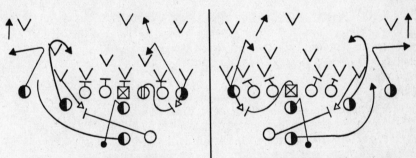

Figure 12-18a: 23 Sprintback | **Figure 12-18b: 22 Sprintback**

FIGURE 12-18: 20 SERIES, SLOT SET PASSES

Figure 12-18a shows a 23 sprintback pass being run against a 52 monster defense. The slot is set to the left. The uncovered right guard pulls to the right to protect the backside, and the fullback blocks to the left from his right half set. The quarterback keys the monster in Easy. The primary targets are the split end with first priority in Easy and the wingback with second priority in the hook area.

The split end has a secondary route to Able which results in a staircase pattern. The tailback flares to the cleared out Easy zone.

Figure 12-18b shows a 22 sprintback pass being run against a split 62 defense. The slot is set to the right. The uncovered center pulls to the left to protect the backside and the fullback blocks to the right from his left half set. The quarterback's focus is on Dog zone. The primary targets are the split end with first priority in Dog and the wingback with second priority in the hook area. The split end has a secondary route to Charlie which results in a staircase pattern. The tailback flares to the cleared out Dog zone.

Figure 12-19 shows 25 and 24 sprintback passes. They are both the same plays with one being run to the left against an even defense and the other being run to the right against an odd defense.

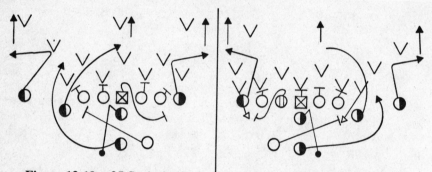

| Figure 12-19a: 25 Sprintback | Figure 12-19b: 24 Sprintback |

FIGURE 12-19: 20 SERIES, SLOT SET PASSES

Figure 12-19a shows a 25 sprintback pass being run against a 44 stack defense. The slot is set to the left. The uncovered center pulls right to protect the backside; the fullback blocks right from his left half set. The quarterback keys the left cornerback in Easy zone. The wingback and split end both run at the cornerback before they cut on their primary routes. The tailback splits the hook area. Both ends and the wingback go to their three-deep zones on secondary routes. The tailback cuts over short middle on his secondary route.

Figure 12-19b shows a 24 sprintback pass being run against a 52 monster defense. The slot is set to the right. The uncovered left guard pulls left to protect the backside; the fullback blocks right from his left half set. The quarterback keys the monster in Dog. The wingback and split end both run at the monster before they cut on their primary routes. The tailback splits the hook area. Both ends and the wingback go to their three deep zones on secondary routes. The tailback cuts over the short middle on his secondary route.

Figure 12-20 shows 27 and 26 sprintback passes. They are both the same with one being run to the left against an even defense and the other being run to the right against an odd defense.

Figure 12-20a shows a 27 sprintback pass being run against a 44 stack

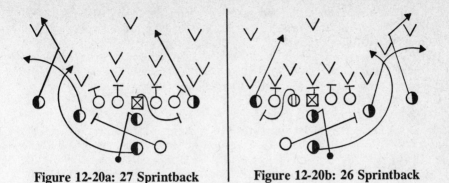

Figure 12-20a: 27 Sprintback | Figure 12-20b: 26 Sprintback

FIGURE 12-20: 20 SERIES, SLOT SET PASSES

defense. The slot is set to the left. The uncovered center pulls to the right to protect the backside, and the fullback blocks to the left from his right half set. The quarterback keys on the cornerback in Easy. The split end cuts off of the cornerback in his route to Able. The wingback is the primary target in Easy. If the cornerback covers him, the quarterback will hit the tailback cutting back over the hook area toward Baker.

Figure 12-20b shows a 26 sprintback pass being run against a 52 monster defense. The slot is set to the right. The uncovered left guard pulls left to protect the backside; the fullback blocks to the right from his right half set. The quarterback keys the monster in Dog. The split end cuts off of the monster in his route to Charlie. The wingback is the primary target in Dog. If the monster covers him, the quarterback will hit the tailback cutting back over the hook area toward Baker.

Figure 12-21 shows 29 and 28 sprintback passes. Again we are sending four deep receivers against deep zone coverages. These plays are both the same with one being run to the left against an odd defense and the other being run to the right against an even defense.

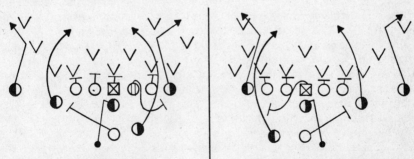

Figure 12-21a: 29 Sprintback | Figure 12-21b: 28 Sprintback

FIGURE 12-21: 20 SERIES, SLOT SET PASSES

Figure 12-21a shows a 29 sprintback pass being run against an Oklahoma 54 defense. The slot is set to the left. The uncovered right guard pulls to the right to protect the backside. The fullback and tailback have switched assignments. The tailback blocks to the left from his fullback set. The split end's route is to outside Able and the tight end's route is to outside Charlie. The wingback splits Able and Baker; the fullback splits Baker and Charlie. The quarterback hits the receiver left open in Baker.

Figure 12-21b shows a 28 sprintout pass being run against a 63 defense. The slot is set to the right. The uncovered center pulls to the left and protects the backside. The fullback and tailback have switched assignments. The tailback blocks to the right from his fullback set. The split end's route is to outside Charlie, and the tight end's route is to outside Able. The wingback splits Charlie and Baker; the fullback splits Able and Baker. The quarterback hits the receiver left open in Baker.

RUNNING THE PATTERNS TO THE BACKSIDE

We use a 90 series sprintback call to run our pass patterns to backside of a slot "T" formation. As with the running plays, the 90 call is a backside series. We only use the 0, 1, 4, 5, 6, 7, 8 and 9 pass patterns with the 90 series. It presents a mirror image which has a reverse effect on the defensive secondary. The basic pass patterns are run away from the set of the slot with a fourth receiver released out of the backfield to the slot side. The tailback is the fourth receiver who is set in the fullback's position. The fullback sets and blocks to the backside which is the same as the pattern side. The uncovered interior lineman pulls from the patterns called and protects the slot side. The quarterback leads to the backside on his sprintback. The big difference is the order of priorities for receivers. The quarterback simply keys the zone to the call and reads through to the backside in order of the first, second, third and fourth priority receivers. He hits the receiver where there is no defensive man. On odd patterns the quarterback reads clockwise Easy to Dog and on even patterns and he reads counterclockwise Dog to Easy. This is easier to do than it may seem. Some of these patterns have been more effective to the backside than they were to the frontside.

Figure 12-22 shows 91 and 90 sprintback passes. They are both the same play with one being run to the left against an odd defense and the other being run to the right against an even defense.

Figure 12-22a shows a 91 sprintback pass being run against a 52 monster defense. The slot is set to the right with the monster playing the slot. The uncovered right guard pulls to the right to protect the slot side. The fullback blocks to the left from his left half set. The quarterback keys Easy and can hit the open tight end in the hook area since the monster is in Dog.

Figure 12-22b shows a 90 sprintback pass being run against a 44 stack defense. The slot is set to the left. The uncovered center pulls to the left and protects the slot side and the fullback blocks right from his right half set. The quarterback begins to read from the right counterclockwise. First priority tight end is covered by the cornerback in Dog's hook area. Second priority wingback

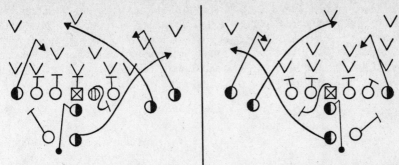

Figure 12-22a: 91 Sprintback | **Figure 12-22b: 90 Sprintback**

FIGURE 12-22: 90 SERIES, SLOT SET PASSES

has a middle linebacker in front of him over the middle. Third priority split end is covered in Easy's hook area. Fourth priority tailback is open in Easy.

Figure 12-23 shows 95 and 94 sprintback passes. They are both the same play with one being run to the left against an even defense and the other being run to the right against an odd defense.

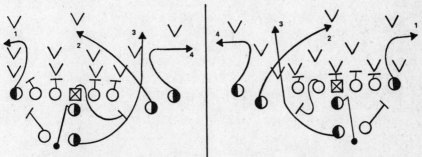

Figure 12-23a: 95 Sprintback | **Figure 12-23b: 94 Sprintback**

FIGURE 12-23: 90 SERIES, SLOT SET PASSES

Figure 12-23a shows a 95 sprintback pass being run against a 44 stack defense. The slot is set to the right. The uncovered center pulls to the right to protect the slot side and the fullback blocks left from his left half set. The quarterback reads from the left clockwise. First, second, and third priorities are covered with the split end open in Easy.

Figure 12-23b shows a 94 sprintback pass being run against a 52 monster defense. The slot is set to the left with the monster playing to the slot. The uncovered left guard pulls left to protect the slot side and the fullback blocks to the right from his right set. The quarterback keys Dog and hits the open tight end since the monster is set in Easy.

Figure 12-24 shows 97 and 96 sprintback passes. They are both the same play with one being run to the left and the other to the right against even defenses.

Figure 12-24a shows a 97 sprintback pass being run against a pro-43 defense. The slot is set to the right with the invert rovers rotated to the slot. The

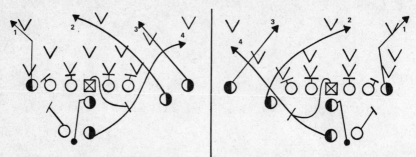

Figure 12-24a: 97 Sprintback　　　**Figure 12-24b: 96 Sprintback**

FIGURE 12-24: 90 SERIES, SLOT SET PASSES

uncovered center pulls right to protect the slot side, and the fullback blocks left from his left half set. The quarterback reads from Easy clockwise to Dog. Either the split end or tailback should be open to the backside.

Figure 12-24b shows a 96 sprintback pass being run against a 44 stack defense. The slot is set to the left. The uncovered center pulls to the left and protects the slot side and the fullback blocks to the right from his right half set. The quarterback reads from Dog counter clockwise to Easy. Either the split end or tailback should be open to the backside.

Figure 12-25 shows 99 and 98 sprintback passes. They are both the same play with one being run to the left and the other to the right against odd defenses.

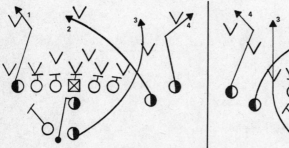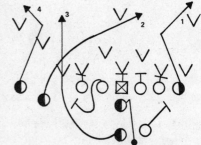

Figure 12-25a: 99 Sprintback　　　**Figure 12-25b: 98 Sprintback**

FIGURE 12-25: 90 SERIES, SLOT SET PASSES

Figure 12-25a shows 99 sprintback pass being run against an eagle 53 defense. The slot is set to the right. The fullback blocks to the left from his left half set. The quarterback reads from Easy clockwise to Dog. The tailback with third priority is open.

Figure 12-25b shows 98 sprintback pass being run against a 52 monster defense. The slot is set to the left. The uncovered left guard pulls to the left and protects the slot side and the fullback blocks to the right from his right half set. The quarterback reads from Dog counter clockwise to Easy. The tailback with third priority is open.

This completes both our basic running and passing systems. Keep in mind that we only select those plays from within the system that fit the characteristics of our personnel, which vary from time to time. When we are behind and time is running out, we need a separate two-minute offense that will get large chunks of yardage in a short time. Next we will cover our quick draw offense.

CHAPTER 13

Shifting From the Power "I" to the Quick Draw Offense

Our multiple power "I" offense has been good to us for scoring touchdowns, staying in the ball game, gaining a lead and controlling the ball to protect a lead. What happens on those occasions when our team is a couple of touchdowns behind, needs considerable yardage and is short of time? If a team does not have a special two-minute offense in reserve, the players will be forced to do things they are not accustomed to doing. If the special catch-up plays are not natural to the team, the players will not have confidence in them. They will often contribute to the opponent's score instead of their own. The odds are against a desperation double-up and catch-up game when the clock is putting pressure on a team that needs large chunks of real estate. The offense must be second nature to the players in order for them to believe in what the coach is trying to do: only then will they believe in themselves. A simple but complete offense is necessary to play catch-up football. We call this our quick draw offense.

A PROVEN "COME FROM BEHIND" OFFENSE

Our quick draw offense has given our spectators some of the most exciting storybook finishes that one can imagine. On a number of occasions we were one to two touchdowns behind at the end of the third quarter. In the fourth quarter our teams scored two to three touchdowns and came from behind to win using the quick draw attack. There were other times when it brought us to within inches of a win, only to have the clock run out. Even at that, we finished by shifting all of the momentum to our side. We had a league football fan that refused to come to our football games until the second half. His reasons were that our games did not get exciting until the fourth quarter, and he could take in the first half of another game. We also had a couple of fans who left our games in disgust at the end of the third quarter when we were down a couple of touchdowns before coming from behind to win.

The first year that we experimented and installed the quick draw offense resulted in a "Cinderella" team far beyond this coach's expectations. It was a year that others regarded our material as just average. Our coaches suspected that our kids had those intangible qualities to spring a couple of big upsets, but we never dreamed we would win the championship. We play in the ever-tough North Suburban League. When a representative from our league does not win the state, they usually decide who does. It's said that there is only a second, a foot or a score in the difference from the top and bottom of our league—there are no breathers.

The following review is of the most satisfying year that this coach has known and will serve as credentials for the quick draw offense. We have all heard that "out of adversity comes greatness." What follows has made a believer out of me.

1. July 1970 was the first year that our State Athletic Association allowed summer camps. It was our first opportunity to experiment, and we had a wonderful team. It is hard to let players with great attitudes keep from from letting your heart overrule your head: as an optimist you look at their pride, but as a realist you could not forget their schedule. We had two weeks with limited abilities and spent one hour a day on basic techniques and offenses. The second hour we spent on innovations. We experimented with a basic innovative five play sequence based on the draw play. It looked so good in that two weeks of summer camp that we adopted it. It had yet to prove itself, but we kept it in reserve to test when the need arose.

2. As we approached our pre-season practice and the opening of school, we were confronted with our first cloud of adversity. School was not to open because we could not get a tax levy passed. We operated on a day-to-day basis through the third week of our schedule, without knowing if each practice was to be our last. We were pressured as "scabs" because we practiced and played when school was not in session. On the eve of our third game the tax levy passed. Never has a group of players so much appreciated the opportunity to play football. Our team was primed to take on Belleville, Illinois, a perennial power from the east side of the river.

3. Our players fought hard but were still behind 8 to 0 with two minutes left in the second quarter when we unveiled our quick draw offense for the first time. We drove 72 yards in nine plays to the eight yard line as the half ended. That two minutes had set the tempo for the second half: we planned to continue with our exploit. We scored, went for two and missed to make the score 8 to 6. They scored to take a 14 to 6 lead into the fourth quarter; then we scored again and came up short again to lose 14 to 12. Afterwards both dressing rooms resembled a morgue. Our 470 yards of offense added to our disappointment. After shaking off the loss and reviewing films, we began to relate the potentials of the quick draw offense to our 470 yards that had only produced 12 points.

4. The following week we opened our league schedule with Normandy, which was considered a contender. They took an early 6 to 0 lead: that score remained until the fourth quarter. We again went to the quick draw offense and scored two touchdowns in the last four minutes to win 13 to 6. This only set the stage for the pandemonium that the quick draw was to cause.

5. In mid-season we played Riverview who was polled number one in the state. They scored early to take a 6 to 0 lead. We began to pick up momentum in the third quarter and kept threatening to pull a 7 to 6 upset. On third down they had a back break loose for an unexpected 95-yard touchdown. Their 13 to 0 lead going into the fourth quarter was a deflating shock. Many had marked us off for a great effort and a loss. This put our players in an emotional fret; they all knew it was quick draw time. We scored three touchdowns in the fourth quarter to upset them 19 to 13. How can I describe the results? I was knocked down from the rush on to the field. There were some from Riverview who had to actually be treated for shock.

6. Our final game was with McCluer for the league championship. It was an anticlimax in view of what had already happened. At the end of the third quarter when McCluer took a 12 to 10 lead, I did not share the optimism our players and fans did. However, as they expected, our quick draw offense scored two touchdowns and we won 23 to 12.

In that total nine game schedule we were in a quick draw situation four times, and it pulled the game out of the fire three times. The next year we were in the final game with McCluer again. This time if they won or tied, they would earn a berth in the state playoffs in which they were favorites to win. They had a 14 to 6 lead on us going into the fourth quarter. Our quick draw offense got us a field goal and a touchdown; we won 16 to 14. It earned us a share of the title and knocked them out of the state.

After that, much interest developed in the area on the quick draw offense. I spoke of it at seminars and clinics and published an article about it. A number of coaches adopted it; one installed it as his basic offense without my blessings. We have found it to be very effective against aggressive penetrating defenses, but our basic offense has been more consistent against technique defenses.

HOW THE QUICK DRAW OFFENSE WAS DEVELOPED

After our 1968 season, we did a lot of soul searching in the off-season. We were not satisfied with being a bridesmaid and never a bride. We had stopped a 20-game winning streak 28 to 19 and tied the state champions 7 to 7, then turned around and lost two straight to teams with losing records. We had always been able to control the ball. When we would get behind in the early stages, we would only make things worse when we tried to catch up. We knew what our problems had been: switching to a specialized two-platoon program would not solve our tactical problem. We did not have a solution.

For no particular reason, I started watching some old singlewing movies featuring the Prinston Bucklateral Series. I was intrigued at how it slowed down the pass rush, and how the buck continued to be effective after the rest of the sequence had been run. The delayed effects would freeze the defense. Then I related between the buck and our draw play. Our draw play would be effective only about once a game if it was called at the right time. To run it a second time was a waste. It was set up by the dropback pass and had a natural delay. Since the buck was the base play, why not substitute the draw as a base play and run the same backfield pattern? The fake of the draw play would slow down the pass rush. This would give us a three-play running sequence, plus all our pass patterns. Adding the screen passes it is a complete offense within itself. Of course, in short yardage situations we mix in our basic tandems and isos. This concept leads to the development of the quick draw offense.

SHIFTING TO FIT OUR PERSONNEL

We run our quick draw offense from a floater "T" backfield set with two split receivers. This requires a shift from the fullhouse power "I" set. The positions in the set that we shift to are determined by our personnel. This involves four players and depends on which of our two ends is the best receiver and if it is our tailback or fullback who is best suited to run the draw. This can vary from year to year. Sometimes our fullback is the best draw man, and other times it is our tailback.

Figure 13-1 shows our shifts when the tailback is our best draw man, and the split end is one of our best primary targets.

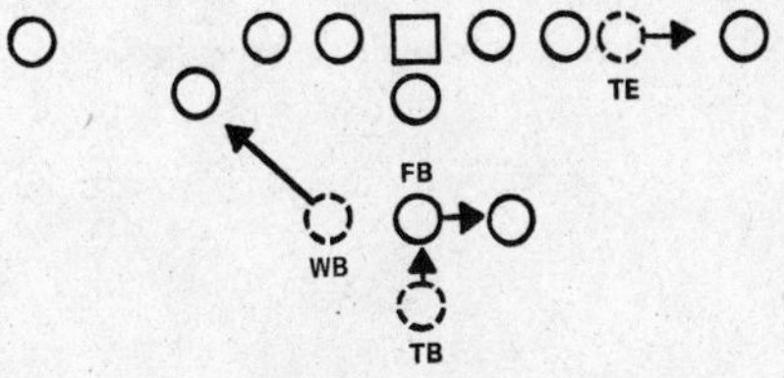

Figure 13-1a: Odd Call 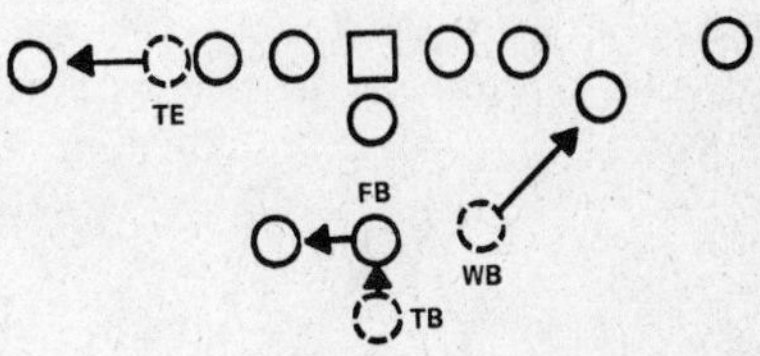   Figure 13-1b: Even Call

FIGURE 13-1: SHIFT FOR TAILBACK DRAWS

Figure 13-1a shows the shift left for an odd call. The wingback shifts from his left half position to a left slot set. The fullback shifts to a right half set, and the tailback shifts into the fullback position. The tight end shifts right to a split set.

Figure 13-1b shows the shift right for an even call. The wingback shifts from his right half position to a right slot set. The fullback shifts to a left half set, and the tailback shifts into a fullback position. The tight end shifts left to a split set.

Figure 13-2 shows our shifts when the fullback is our best draw man and the tight end is one of our best primary targets.

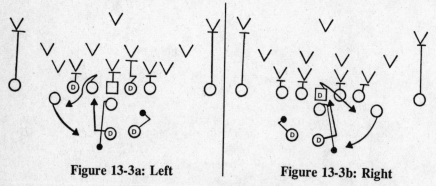

Figure 13-2a: Odd Call   Figure 13-2b: Even Call

FIGURE 13-2: SHIFT FOR FULLBACK DRAWS

Figure 13-2a shows the shift left for an odd call. The wingback shifts from left half position to a left slot set. The tailback shifts to a right half set and the tight end shifts left to a split set.

Figure 13-2b shows the shift right for an even call. The wingback shifts from his right half position to a right slot set. The tailback shifts to a left half set and the tight end shifts right to a split set.

THE BASIC DRAW SYSTEM

Figure 13-3. All plays in the quick draw offense are basically the same: they are based on the fullback draw. Basically the same blocking scheme is used for both the running and passing plays. We use our pass blocking scheme as shown in Chapter 11 (Figure 11-7). The only difference is that we pull the uncovered interior lineman to the call instead of using him to the backside. All of the plays are based on a two-count delay at four positions. This is the time it should take for the quarterback to reach his waiting draw back. Our uncovered interior linemen to the call take two-count delays by showing pass. Our tailback takes an

Figure 13-3a: Left   Figure 13-3b: Right

FIGURE 13-3: THE BASIC DRAW SYSTEM

aggressive step to the backside with a two-count delay before leading through the hole. The fullback takes a jab step to the frontside and delays until the quarterback reaches him. He then takes the ball or the fake and runs through the uncovered lineman to the call side. On odd defenses it would be over the front-side guard; on even defenses it would be over the center.

Figure 13-3a shows the quick draw set to the left for an odd call against an odd defense. The uncovered guards show pass. The left guard pulls left after the delay. The tailback jab steps to the right with his two-count delay. The fullback jab steps to the left and waits for the quarterback. Then he either runs the ball or the fakes over the left guard.

Figure 13-3b shows the quick draw set to the right for an even call against an even defense. The uncovered center shows pass and then pulls right after the delay. The tailback jab steps to the left with his two-count delay. The fullback jab steps to the right and waits for the quarterback. He then either runs the ball or fakes over the center.

THE QUICK DRAW RUNNING SEQUENCE

Figure 13-4. There are three basic running plays in the quick draw sequence. Running them to both sides makes a total of six running plays. The order of the running sequence is as follows: the first play is the fullback draw. The second play is to fake the draw and run the wingback counter. The third play is to fake the counter and run the quarterback draw. Next we will look at this sequence to both the left and right.

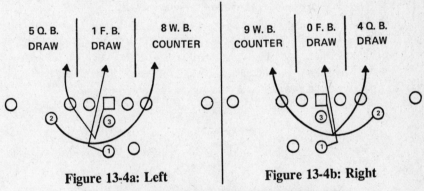

Figure 13-4a: Left   Figure 13-4b: Right

FIGURE 13-4: THE RUNNING SEQUENCE

Figure 13-4a shows the three-play draw sequence being run to the left. The first play is the basic "1 fullback draw." The second play is the "8 wingback counter" with a fake fullback draw. The slot must be set from the call. The third play is the "5 quarterback draw" with the counter fake.

Figure 13-4b shows the same three-play draw sequence being run to the right. The first play is "0 fullback draw," which is basic. The second play is the "9 wingback counter" with a fake fullback draw. The slot is set from the call. The third play is "4 quarterback draw" with a counter fake.

Since the whole quick draw offense is based on the fake of the fullback draw, we need to examine the techniques between the quarterback and fullback.

The fullback takes one exaggerated lead step toward the flanker with his inside arm parallel to his chin and waits for the quarterback. The quarterback takes the snap and immediately flashes the ball to his ear. He lets everyone see him put the ball into the waiting fullback's numbers while his back is to the defense. The fullback covers over the ball and pushes off of his lead foot toward his uncovered interior lineman. The quarterback can either leave the ball or pull it out and continue his fade.

Next we will show all three basic running plays of the quick draw sequence run to both the left and right against odd and even defense.

THE BASIC FULLBACK DRAW PLAYS

The fullback draw plays are the base for the entire quick draw offense; *Figure 13-5* shows these plays run to the left and right:

1. The split receivers and the flanker run at a controlled speed as if they are running a pass pattern; then they mirror block the three-deep secondary.

2. The covered interior linemen block the men out from the point-of-attack. This includes uncovered tackles who also block out.

3. The uncovered interior lineman shows pass for a two-count delay and then blocks the near backside linebacker from the call.

4. The point-of-attack is over the uncovered lineman.

5. The tailback takes his two-count delay, runs through the uncovered lineman and blocks the first man off the line of scrimmage to show from the frontside.

6. The fullback maintains his delay until the quarterback places the ball in his stomach; then he runs over the set of his uncovered lineman.

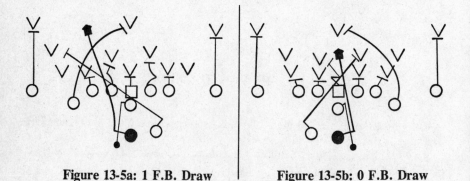

Figure 13-5a: 1 F.B. Draw | Figure 13-5b: 0 F.B. Draw

FIGURE 13-5: BASIC FULLBACK DRAWS

Figure 13-5a shows a "1 fullback draw" being run against a 52 monster defense. The left guard is the uncovered lineman and shows pass with delay before blocking the linebacker. The tailback takes a quick jab step right before running through his left guard to block the frontside man off the line of scrimmage who is the monster. The fullback takes his jab step left and waits for the ball before carrying it over his left guard.

Figure 13-5b shows a "0 fullback draw" being run against a 44 stack defense. The center is the uncovered lineman and shows pass with delay before blocking the first backside defensive man off the line of scrimmage. The tailback takes a jab step to the left before running through center and blocking the frontside linebacker. The fullback takes his jab step right and waits for the ball before carrying it over center.

All the following plays of the quick draw offense will fake this fullback draw before they are completed. After these plays are successfully run, we can come back to the fullback draw effectively.

THE WINGBACK COUNTER PLAYS

The wingback counters are run after faking the fullback draws. The slot sets must be shifted from the calls. *Figure 13-6* shows these plays run to the left and the right. They work like the old "statute-of-liberty."

1. Everything is basically the same for the covered interior linemen and split ends.
2. The uncovered interior linemen take their delays by showing pass before pulling and blocking the first defensive player who shows to the call.
3. The tailback takes his two-count delay until his pulling uncovered lineman is clear, and then leads through the hole to seal.
4. The fullback fakes the draw before the hand-off to the wingback. The timing is natural.

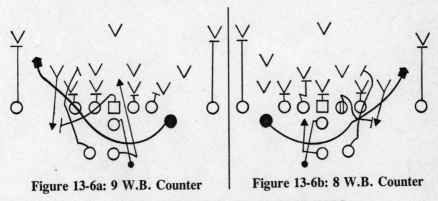

Figure 13-6a: 9 W.B. Counter   Figure 13-6b: 8 W.B. Counter

FIGURE 13-6: WINGBACK COUNTERS

Figure 13-6a shows a "9 wingback counter" being run against a 44 stack defense. The center is the uncovered lineman and pulls left to block the first defensive player out who shows. The tailback jab steps to the left and waits for his pulling center to clear before leading through the hole and sealing. The quarterback fakes the fullback draw to his right before handing to the wingback going to the left.

Figure 13-6b shows an "8 wingback counter" being run against a 52 monster defense. The right guard is the uncovered lineman who pulls right to block the first defensive player who shows. The tailback jab steps to the right and waits for his pulling right guard to clear before leading through the hole and sealing. the quarterback fakes the fullback draw to his left before handing to the wingback going to the right.

We have found that these counters are more effective than most reverse plays because we can repeat them with success when mixing them in with other quick draw plays.

THE QUARTERBACK DRAW PLAYS

The quarterback draw plays are run after faking the wingback counters. The quarterback only needs to be concerned about faking the fullback draw play while his back is to the defense. The wingback is to do the faking for him. All the quarterback has to do is follow him with his head. Once the wingback is clear, the quarterback then pivots back through the hole. *Figure 13-7* shows these plays being run to both the left and right.

1. Everything is basically the same for all the interior linemen and both split ends.
2. The tailback takes a quick delay before leading through the hole to seal.
3. The quarterback fakes the draw to fullback.
4. The wingback fakes the counter, and then the quarterback pivots through the hole.

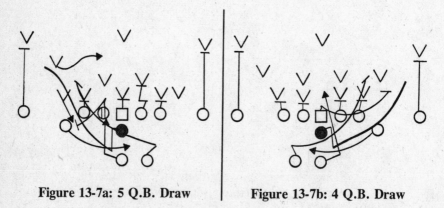

Figure 13-7a: 5 Q.B. Draw   Figure 13-7b: 4 Q.B. Draw

FIGURE 13-7: QUARTERBACK DRAWS

Figure 13-7a shows a "5 quarterback draw" being run against a 52 monster defense. The monster goes with the wingback's fake. The left guard is the uncovered lineman who pulls left to block the first defensive player to show. The tailback takes a quick jab step to the right before leading through the hole. After the wingback fakes right, the quarterback pivots through the 5 hole.

Figure 13-7b shows a "4 quarterback draw" being run agaisnt a 44 stack defense. The center is the uncovered lineman who pulls right and blcoks the first defensive player to show. The tailback takes a quick jab step to the left before leading through the hole. After the wingback fakes left, the quarterback pivots through the 4 hole.

These plays work like a spinner play from the singlewing. Only occasionally use these plays after they have been set up by the rest of the running sequence.

Now that we have established the quick draw running sequence, we will look at the quick draw passing attack. We use sideline screen passes and dropback passes from which we run all our patterns.

THE SCREEN PASSES

Almost all offenses have sideline screen passes. Our using it with a fake draw has made it more effective and consistent. There are three reasons for this. First, the fake of the fullback draw up the middle hides the development of the screen. Second, the guard, tackle and backs from the call carry out their basic assignments and protect the quarterback's fake and fade to the backside. Third, the tackle, guard and center who form the screens to the call have definite responsibilities. They slide off their defensive contacts to the inside and around them before forming on the tackle who set the screen to the outside. The tackle has the outside, the guard has the seem, and the center protects the backside. This prevents confusion and keeps a defensive player from slipping through the screen, as often happens.

We use both the tailback and wingback as receivers in our sideline screens. The tailback takes his jab step delay and waits for the outside defensive rusher to clear his outside shoulder before setting up behind his guard. The wingback goes downfield and curls back between the tackle and guard to set up behind the screen. He yells "Go" after receiving the ball. Next we will show wingback and tailback screen passes being run to both sides.

Figure 13-8 shows a 9 wingback screen pass being run to the left and an 8 wingback screen pass being run to the right. The slot sets, fake draws and screens are all three to the frontside.

Figure 13-8a. The interior linemen to the right protect the backside, and the interior linemen to the left set their screen to the frontside. The fake fullback draw is to the left. The tailback blocks to the left behind the fake after his delay. The wingback curls in Easy before setting up behind the screen.

Figure 13-8b. The interior line to the left protects the backside; the interior line to the right set their screen to the frontside. The fake fullback draw is to the right. The tailback blocks to the right behind the fake after his delay. The wingback curls in Dog before setting up behind the screen.

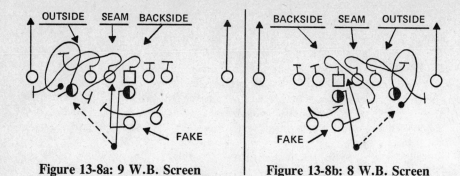

Figure 13-8a: 9 W.B. Screen | Figure 13-8b: 8 W.B. Screen

FIGURE 13-8: WINGBACK SCREEN PASSES

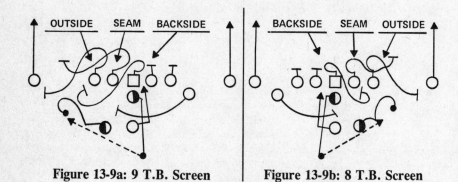

Figure 13-9a: 9 T.B. Screen | Figure 13-9b: 8 T.B. Screen

FIGURE 13-9: TAILBACK SCREEN PASSES

Figure 13-9 shows a 9 tailback screen pass being run to the left and an 8 tailback screen pass being run to the right. The fake draws are run to the frontside toward the slot sets; the screens are set to the backside.

Figure 13-9a. The interior linemen to the right protect the frontside and the interior linemen to the left set their screen to the backside. The fake fullback draw is to the right. The wingback goes left to the backside to block behind the fake. The tailback delays to the left until the defensive end clears his outside shoulder; then he sets up behind the screen.

Figure 13-9b. The interior linemen to the left protect the frontside and the interior linemen to the right set their screen to the backside. The fake fullback draw is to the left. The wingback goes right to the backside to block behind the fake. The tailback takes his delay to the right until the defensive end clears his outside shoulder. He then sets-up behind the screen.

THE DROPBACK PASSES

The term "dropback" is synomymous with draw. The reason we do not use the term "draw pass" is to prevent confusion with a draw play call in the huddle. "Drop back" means to fake the draw before the quarterback fades into the pocket which is formed by the pulling frontside uncovered lineman and the backside tailback. The dropback passes are more effective with our deep patterns than any other backfield action. This is because the delay of our fake draw slows down the pass rush and gives the patterns more time to develop. All of our pass patterns can be run with our dropback action.

Figure 13-10 shows our dropback pass action being run to both sides. All of our odd patterns are run out of a slot set to the left; all even patterns are run out of a slot set to the right.

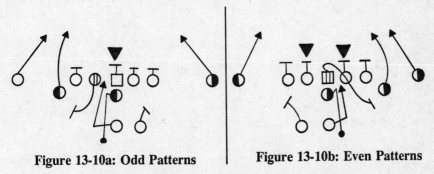

Figure 13-10a: Odd Patterns | Figure 13-10b: Even Patterns

FIGURE 13-10: THE DROP BACK PASSES

Figure 13-10a shows the backfield set left for odd pattern calls against odd defenses. The left guard delays and pulls to the left to protect the frontside and the tailback protects the right backside. The quarterback fakes the fullback draw to the left before fading into the pocket.

Figure 13-10b shows the backfield set right for even pattern calls against even defenses. The uncovered center delays and pulls to the right to protect the frontside and the tailback protects the left back side. The quarterback fakes the fullback draw to the right before fading into the pocket.

Next we will show all of our pass patterns being run with these dropback actions to both the left and the right.

Figure 13-11 shows our 1 and 0 dropback pass patterns being run against both odd and even defenses.

Figure 13-11a shows 1 dropback pass being run against a 52 monster defense. The left guard pulls and protects the left frontside and the tailback protects the right backside. The quarterback fakes the fullback draw to his left before fading into the pocket. The primary targets both make their moves off the monster. They are the wingback who has the route to Easy flat, and the frontside end who has Easy hook area. Since the monster is in Easy zone, the Dog zone is open. The quarterback hits the backside end in Dog hook area.

Figure 13-11b shows 0 dropback pass being run against a 44 stack defense. The uncovered center pulls and protects the right frontside, and the tailback protects the left backside. The quarterback fakes the fullback draw to his right before fading into the pocket. The primary targets both make their moves off the cornerback. They are the wingback, who has the route to Dog flat, and the

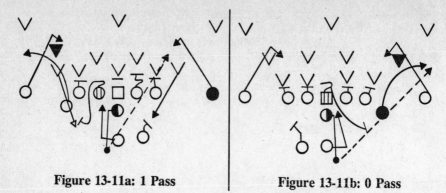

Figure 13-11a: 1 Pass   Figure 13-11b: 0 Pass

FIGURE 13-11: 1 AND 0 DROPBACKS

strongside end, who has the Dog hook area. Since the cornerback covers the end in the hook area, the quarterback hits the wingback in the flat.

Figure 13-12 shows our drag and go dropback pass patterns being run against both odd and even defenses.

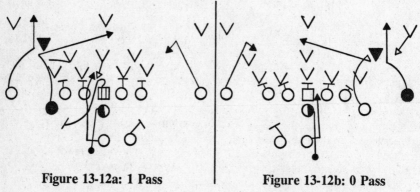

Figure 13-12a: 1 Pass   Figure 13-12b: 0 Pass

FIGURE 13-12: DRAG AND GO DROPBACKS

Figure 13-12a shows 1 drag and go dropback pass being run against a 43-pro defense. The uncovered center pulls to the left to protect the frontside; the tailback protects the right backside. The quarterback fakes the fullback draw to the left before fading into the pocket. The wingback has the drag pattern and the frontside end has the go pattern to Able zone. The drag man is the quarterback's best target.

Figure 13-12b shows 0 drag and go dropback pass being run against a 53 eagle defense. There are no uncovered linemen to pull; all that is necessary is for the right tackle to block out. The tailback protects the left backside. The quarter-back fakes the full back draw to the right before fading. The primary targets are in Dog zone. The wingback has the drag pattern and the frontside end has the go pattern to Charlie zone. The go man is the quarterback's best target.

Figure 13-13 shows our go and drag dropback pass patterns being run against both odd and even defenses:

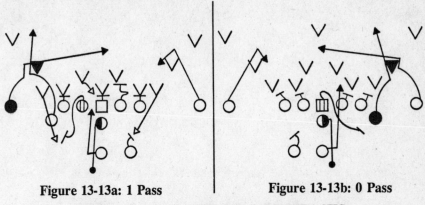

Figure 13-13a: 1 Pass   Figure 13-13b: 0 Pass

FIGURE 13-13: GO AND DRAG DROPBACKS

Figure 13-13a shows 1 go and drag dropback pass being run against a 54 Oklahoma defense. The uncovered left guard pulls to the left to protect the frontside and the tailback protects the right backside. The quarterback fakes the fullback draw to the left before fading into the pocket. The primary targets are in Easy zone. The wingback has the go pattern to Able, and the strongside end has the drag pattern. The drag man is the quarterback's best target.

Figure 13-13b shows 0 go and drag dropback pass being run against a split 44 defense. The uncovered center pulls to the right to protect the frontside and the tailback protects the left backside. The quarterback fakes the fullback draw to the right before fading into the pocket. The primary targets are in Dog zone. The wingback has the go pattern to Charlie and the strongside end has the drag pattern. The go pattern is the quarterback's best target.

Figure 13-14 shows our 3 and 2 dropback pass patterns being run against both odd and even defenses:

Figure 13-14a shows 3 dropback pass being run against a split 62 defense. The uncovered center pulls to left to protect the frontside, and the tailback protects the right backside. The quarterback fakes the fullback draw to the left before fading into the pocket. The primary targets are in Easy zone. The wingback has the hook area, and the strongside end has the left flat. Both ends could be the open receivers for the quarterback.

Figure 13-14b shows 2 dropback pass being run against a 53 eagle defense. There is no uncovered interior lineman, and the tailback protects the left backside. The quarterback fakes the fullback draw to the right before fading. The primary targets are in Dog zone. The wingback has the hook area, and the strongside end has the right flat. The right end is the quarterback's best target.

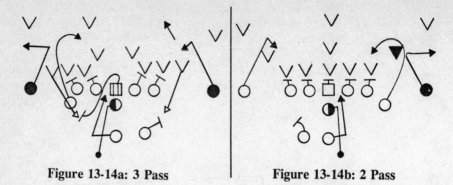

Figure 13-14a: 3 Pass   Figure 13-14b: 2 Pass

FIGURE 13-14: 3 AND 2 DROPBACKS

Figure 13-15 shows our 5 and 4 dropback pass patterns being run against both odd and even defenses.

Figure 13-15a shows 5 dropback pass being run against a 52 monster defense. The uncovered left guard pulls to the left to protect the frontside and the tailback protects the backside to the right. The quarterback fakes the fullback draw to the left before fading into the pocket. The primary targets are in Easy zone. Since the monster is covering Easy zone, the open receiver is the backside end in Dog zone.

Figure 13-15b shows 4 dropback pass being run against a 43-pro defense. The uncovered center pulls right to protect the frontside and the tailback protects the backside to the left. The quarterback fakes the fullback draw to the right before fading into the pocket. The primary targets are in Dog zone. The wingback has his route over the short middle; the frontside end has the flat. The wingback is the quarterback's best target.

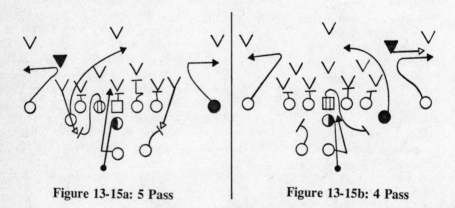

Figure 13-15a: 5 Pass   Figure 13-15b: 4 Pass

FIGURE 13-15: 5 AND 3 DROPBACKS

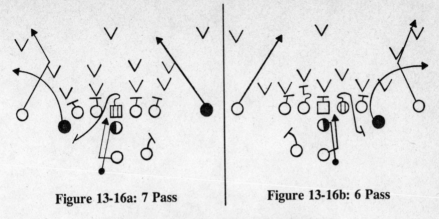

Figure 13-16a: 7 Pass | **Figure 13-16b: 6 Pass**

FIGURE 13-16: 7 AND 6 DROPBACKS

Figure 13-16 shows our 7 and 6 dropback pass patterns being run against both odd and even defenses.

Figure 13-16a shows 7 dropback pass being run against a 44 stack defense. The uncovered center pulls to the left to protect the frontside and the tailback protects the backside to the right. The quarterback fakes the fullback draw to the left before fading into the pocket. The primary targets are to the left. The frontside end is in Able zone and the wingback is in Easy zone. Either the wingback or the backside end should be open.

Figure 13-16b shows 6 dropback pass being run against a 52 monster defense. The uncovered right guard pulls right to protect the frontside and the tailback protects the backside to the left. The quarterback fakes the draw play to the right before fading into the pocket. The primary targets are to the right. The frontside end is to Charlie zone and the wingback is in Dog zone. The wingback should be the quarterback's best target.

We do not recommend the use of 8 and 9 patterns with the dropback passing attack.

The quick draw offense has been the most exciting tactical adventure that we have experienced. With your reading of this Chapter, I hope that you have been able to share some of our enthusiasm. With all good conscience I cannot but recommend that you adapt the quick draw sequence as a supplement to your own basic offense. We feel that it could be simply applied to almost any offensive system. You could use your own numbering system or pass patterns. The running sequence could be run out of a split backfield set and "I" set, a floater "T" set or a flanker "T" set. You probably have one of these backfield sets with a draw play in your system. The draw would be the base for you to build your own quick draw offense.

CHAPTER 14

A Conclusion for the Multiple Power "I" Offense

We use a specialized two-platoon system to program our multiple power "I." The term "program" needs to be put into its proper perspective: there are some who do not realize the difference between the terms "team" and "program." A team is a specific phase and result of a program. With good conditions it takes three years to build a team. A team graduates only to be rebuilt again. Graduations do not effect good programs: they replenish themselves from one level to the next. With a good program the so-called rebuilding year may not be the best, but it will produce a winner. If the situation is right, it takes five years to build a good program. It takes longer to build a program than to build a team. Instant success is not lasting success: only your evaluation of your situation can determine the program you need.

SPECIALIZING WITH A TWO-PLATOON SYSTEM

The two-platoon system has long been accepted at college and pro levels as the best for programming and organizing. An unbelievable number of large high schools across this country shy away from two-platoon specialization. You will hear their coaches say they do not have enough good players, and that they are always going to put their eleven best on field. Some coaches find more security in the talent of their players than their coaching abilities: this can waste much of their own resources and time. For many years I was one of those coaches. After a strong start and a very disappointing finish one year, I changed. Our program netted championship results in the second year. A number of seniors with limited abilities became so well schooled in their techniques they were able to out-finesse more talented opponents. Players with physical limitations starting for us could not have started for some of the opponents we were beating. We soon increased our player participation from 90 to 150 playing three schedules at three levels, and this did not include our two freshman teams. We carried an 80-man traveling squad: forty on an offensive bus and 40 on a defensive bus. We were accused of taking our own snake-pit with us. It goes without saying that we had to be highly organized. Platoon specialization cuts your organizational problems in half. Because our situations are all different, there is no point in going into the organization of our program.

There is a much smaller situation I would like to use as an example to make my point. Bill Green, our defensive secondary coach, and I were attending a State Football Clinic. We sat in on a session where the speaker's team had just won the medium-small class state championship. We could not believe that this coach was talking about platoon specialization. We later heard other coaches say that he must be crazy. Bill and I did not want to talk to them. We wanted to talk to this guy who was crazy enough to win the state. We approached him and introduced ourselves. This lead to the most interesting and amazing pigskin session that we could imagine. His school was located in a small Missouri town with about 500-plus enrollment in the top four grades. They had five coaches for three levels. All the staff varsity coaches specialized in an offense or defensive phase. The players practiced and played either offense or defense. Each coach worked with only those boys at all three levels who specialized in his phase. As an example, the offensive backfield coach worked with the varsity, the "B" team and the freshman backs. In the second year the number of boys out for football doubled. This coach was not crazy: he just had a lot of guts, and won the state because of it. This coach's parting words were, "I can not understand why all big schools do not platoon." We had no answer because we didn't either. I'm not sure I would have guts enough to platoon if I were coaching in a school of his size.

DOUBLING THE RESULTS IN HALF THE TIME

We had success with the multiple power "I" when we used our best eleven, and felt that that was all they could put on the field at once. Their success was inconsistent, however. The offense is only one of three phases of football. The offense, defense and kicking game are all equally important and dependent on one another. Our best players had three times as much to learn and we only had half the amount of time to teach them as we do now with the platoon system. The good players became much more effective in learning, practicing and playing just one phase. The marginal players got the job done and are happy to have the opportunity that they otherwise would not have had. We have doubled our time to teach half as much. With a platoon program, we have improved and expanded the execution of our multiple power "I" offense.

Let us now examine the advantages of a specialized two-platoon program:

1. It gives better organization and utilization of time.
2. It specializes coaches and helps them to know and to evaluate personnel better.
3. It gives players an opportunity to identify with a coach, so that they do not feel lost in the shuffle.

4. It gives twice the number of players the opportunity to play.
5. It cuts down on injuries and mental fatigue.
6. It cuts the learning situation and mistakes in half.
7. It helps maintain control when things go wrong.
8. It helps keep everyone busy and satisfied.

The large schools' problem is not the inability to get enough players out to platoon. If they get the coaching staffs, schedules and administrative backing, they should get the players they need within the second year of a platoon program.

THE FOLLOW-UP

Athletes present the best follow-up opportunities in education. They often come back after graduation. The greatest satisfaction a coach can have is when his players come back to let him know how they are doing and to say thanks. Only a small percentage of them go on to play at the college level. As a coach you have the following obligations to give them assistance and guidance with recruitment:

1. Help the athlete to understand and recognize his own potential and limitations so that he can make his own choice.
2. Help the parents to understand the two-way recruiting process so that they may help their boy in making his choice.
3. Cooperate with all recruiters who employ a professional approach.
4. Make it clear to all parties concerned that the high school coach's role is to give assistance upon request by either party concerned—but not to influence either's decision.

Athletic recruitment involves four different parties with different concerns. These are the athletes, parents, recruiters and high school coaches. It is important that we define the role of each:

1. *Athletes* receive financial aid from the higher institutions that they represent and contribute their talents to. Their participation is usually for fun and prestige.
2. *Parents* view it as a means to the end: the end result is a college education.
3. *Recruiters* are the college coaches or field representative who are responsible to obtain the athletes that will help their teams to *win!*
4. *High school coaches* are simply the counselors or mediators: they are in the middle and assist both parties in getting together. After that they should fade into the background.

If athletes could be categorized on their high school, size, ability, looks, speed, mental aptitude, personalities, etc., recruitment would be simple, but because they are still in the stage of developing, and because of the many intangible human qualities, big time football recruiters work on the volume basis.

They say if one of the three athletes they recruit makes it, they have done an above-average job.

We receive an estimated seventy-plus form letters a year from colleges requesting recruitment information. We answer them all with a recruiting form letter which gives our players a broad exposure. Many recruiters have told us we are among the very few that do this, and that it would be an advantage to all concerned if everyone did.

A SATISFYING CONCLUSION

Both our multiple power "I" and the quick draw offense have proven to be very successful. Because of the multiple characteristics there should be a number of phases presented in this book which fit into almost anyone's situation. The more specialized you are, the most multiple you can make your offense. You should limit your multiple application to only those phases that naturally fit your situation, personnel and the time in which you have to work. The glossary which follows will serve you as a point of reference.

Glossary

Able Zone The left deep third of the defensive secondary.

Backfield Techniques The elements used in putting three basic backfield maneuvers into action.

Backside Calls When the backfield is set strong from the point of attack.

Backside Series When the play or sequence is run from the side on which the wingback is set.

Baker Zone The middle deep third of the defensive secondary.

Balanced Line When there are three men on the line of scrimmage to each side of center.

Belly Series The three-play option sequence based on a fake ride of the fullback.

Bifocal Series A four-play running sequence.

Blocking Rules The system for three basic types of blocking assignments.

Blocking Terms The ten basic words that are used in the integration of the basic triad blocking rules.

Bootleg A term to designate a pass or run sequence to the backside.

Buck Lateral A term that describes a four-play running sequence run from a single wing.

Bump and Run A defensive technique used on an eligible receiver immediately after the snap.

Call The signal that designates a play or set.

Call Man The lead blocker to the inside of the hole that is designated by the second digit in the call.

Charlie Zone The right deep third of the defensive secondary.

Check and Release A technique for backside offensive linemen to force defensive players to their outside shoulders before going down field to block.

Clear Out When a primary receiver takes his secondary route to a deep zone, leaving the short zone open for a secondary receiver.

Corner Back The linebackers outside of ends off the line of scrimmage.

Counter The second play of the quick draw sequence that is an outgrowth of the old "Statue-of-Liberty" play.

Covered Linemen Offensive interior linemen with a defensive down lineman on them.

Cut-Back A maneuver by a ball carrier in which he turns head on against the defensive pursuit.

Cut-Off A blocking term for an offensive lineman who applies a technique to fill the hole to his inside that was left by a pulling lineman.

Daylight An opening for a ball carrier in the defensive front.

Defensive Tendencies The strong and weak characteristics of the defense.

Delay A two-count hesitation applied by the uncovered interior linemen and backs in the quick draw offense.

Deployment Shifting offensive players from their basic positions to a secondary set.

Dog Zone The right short half of the defensive secondary.

Double Team A general term that can either be applied to tandem or post and lead blocking. It can also be applied to two-on-one situations such as the option.

Drag and Go An inside and long pass pattern applied by two primary receivers, adapted from a basketball screen maneuver.

Draw Delayed running plays following a fake dropback pass.

Dropback The basic backfield maneuver for the quick draw passing attack.

Easy Zone The left short half of the defensive secondary.

Even Defense Has an uncovered center.

Even Holes The second digits in the call that indicate the points-of-attack to the right for ball carriers.

Even Patterns The second digits in the call that indicate the pass patterns to the right.

Even Series The first digits in the call that indicates the backfield sets to the splitside of a balanced line or the shortside of an unbalanced line.

Fifth (Man) Defensive men to key for reading the defense.

Finesse One of three tactical characteristics that put emphasis on consistent execution.

Flanker A secondary frontside set for the wingback to the outside of his end.

Flat The outside areas of the short zones.

Flip-Flop Either linemen or backs to exchange the set of their basic positions from one side to the other.

Floater The secondary frontside set for a wingback either as a slot or flanker.

Formation The set of all the offensive players.

Frontside Calls When the backfield is set strong to the point-of-attack.

Frontside Series When the play or sequence is run to the side on which the wingback is set.

Fullhouse Backfield Set When all three running backs are set in their basic positions.

Game Plan A tactical format based on opponents' tendencies.

Gap A defensive down set between two offensive players.

Goal Line Defense Short yardage defenses.

Go and Drag A long and inside pass pattern applied by two primary receivers, adapted from a basketball screen maneuver.

Hole Offensive point-of-attack designated by the second digit.

Hook A short inside pass pattern.

Hook Area The inside of the short key.

Influence An offensive maneuver to give a false key to lead a defensive player from the play.

Inside Linebacker Any linebackers set between our two offensive tackles.

Inside Gap A frontside blocking term used in all blocking rules.

Invert Rotation A defensive maneuver by two inside defensive backs adjusting to sets or backfield flow.

Isolation (iso) A blocking rule and backfield technique related to tandems.

Jab Step A quick lead step with delay.

Keying Watching an assigned opponent to determine set and reaction.

Lead Block A term and technique done by the call man who blocks the first defensive man to the inside or off the L.O.S.

L.O.S. Line of scrimmage.

Man-to-Man Matching up players in defensive coverage.

Mirror Block A blocking technique used by the split end.

Monster A roving defensive linebacker playing the strongside of the offense.

Multiple Elements Many integrated techniques and formations.

N.L.B. Near linebacker closest to point-of-attack.

Non Rhythm Count A delay between each phase of the snap signal to prevent mistakes because of anticipation.

Odd Defense Has a covered center.

Odd Holes The second digit in the call that indicates the point-of-attack to the left for ball carriers.

Odd Patterns The second digit in the call that indicates the pass patterns to the left.

Odd Series The second digit in the call that indicates the backfield set to the tight side of a balanced line or the strong side of an unbalanced line.

On A triad blocking term in the application of all blocking rules.

Option An offensive maneuver to put two offensive men on one defensive man, and then making a choice.

Outside Gap A backside blocking term used in all blocking rules.

Overshifted A term applied to the defense when they have shifted down one full man against an unbalanced line.

Passing Tree All the pass patterns and calls for an individual receiver set in a certain position.

Patterns The route for a receiver on a single pass pattern.

Pitch-Out Lateral the ball to another player.

Pivot The technique of an individual turning on the ball of his jab foot before his execution.

Platoon A term applied to specialized programming of two teams for two phases.

Playaction A term to designate a pass after the faking of the power techniques.

Play-the-Game The short yardage offense.

Pocket Pass blockers in a concave set in the backfield for pass protection.

Point-of-Attack The hole in the line designated by the second digit of the call.

Post Block A term and technique in tandem rules that applies to the first offensive lineman to the inside of the call man in a double team situation.

Power One of three tactical characteristics the puts emphasis on strength.

Power Rules A basic type of blocking assignment for the fullback option sequence.

Power Techniques Used by the backfield in the fullback option sequence.

Primary Targets The first in choice of two pass receivers working on one defender.

Priority An order for a running sequence or pass pattern.

Program A long-range format for consistency in producing good teams.

Pull or Puller Applies to an offensive interior lineman who pulls behind his own line to trap or seal.

Pump A fake action with the passing arm.

Pursuit A reaction angle of defensive players to keep the ball carrier between them and the side line past the line of scrimmage.

Quick Draw A general term applied to a two-minute offense.

Reach Both an offensive and defensive term applied to a lineman assigned to make contact on his adjacent lineman's opponent. Applied in sweep blocking rules.

Reading Anticipating the opponent's team maneuvers through individual keys.

Reverse The third play to the backside that is applied with the sweep-slant sequence.

Reverse Pivot To lead from the call making a full turn in one motion before execution.

Rover Synonymous with monster.

Scramble A secondary blocking technique.

Seal Block A blocking term for the first man outside the call to block the first inside defensive man off the line of scrimmage.

Secondary The defensive backfield.

Secondary Target The second in choice of pass receivers.

Sequence A backfield pattern where all plays look alike, the only difference being in who gets the ball.

Series The first digits in the call that indicate the sequence and sets.

Set The secondary position before the snap.

Shift Used by the backfield to get from their basic position to a secondary set before the snap.

Short Punt A supplementary offensive formation that was used with the single wing. It used a cross spinner and trap sequence.

Shortside To the weakside of an unbalanced line.

Signal Calls at the line of scrimmage to designate the snap.

Single Wing A very popular offense perfected during the 20s and 30s. The formation did not have a quarterback under center and required a direct snap to the fullback or tailback. It was run behind both balanced and unbalanced lines and featured double team blocking.

Slant A backfield technique used in the sweep sequence where the fullback takes a hand-off over tackle from a halfback set from the call.

Slot A secondary set for the wingback between his split end and tackle.

Snap Putting the ball into play at the line of scrimmage.

Specialization A player concentrating on but one phase of the game.

Speed One of three tactical characteristics that puts emphasis on quickness.

Spinner A backfield maneuver from the singlewing or short punt.

Split Side The side of a balanced line to which the split end is set.

Split "T" A very popular offense that was developed during the 40s.

Sprintback A term to designate a pass from a sweep backfield action using a fourth receiver without a fake.

Stack A defensive linebacker set directly behind his down lineman.

Stair Case A pass pattern in which the receiver runs a square-out to the flat, and then cuts straight up the field when the quarterback pumps.

Statue-of-Liberty The classical fake pass and wide reverse.

Strategy A tactical plan of attack.

Strongside To the long side of the unbalanced line.

Sweep A play using pulling guards and a flanker to get wide.

Sweep Rules A basic type of blocking rules used with sweep and slant plays.

Sweep Techniques Used by the backfield to get wide.

System Tactical methods.

Tandem A double team blocking technique used by two backs to the outside of the hole.

Tandem Rules A basic type of blocking assignments to double team and isolate at the hole.

Targets Two pass receivers working on one defender.

Techniques Method of execution.

Tight Side The side of a balanced line to which the tight end is set.

Trap A blocking maneuver to take a defensive player out after he was allowed to penetrate the hole. Related to the tandem rules.

Triad A single technique or term being applied to three sets of blocking rules.

Triple Option The quarterback and fullback two-on-one the defensive tackle with the belly option. The quarterback then options the keep or pitchout off the defensive end.

Unbalanced Line When there are four men on the line of scrimmage to one side of center and two to the other side.

Uncovered Linemen Offensive interior linemen with no defensive down linemen on them.

Undershifted When the defensive interior line make no adjustment to an unbalanced line.

Walk Away A set adjustment of defensive ends to the split side of a balanced line or the shortside of an unbalanced line.

Wingback The name of a position for which the basic sets are halfback and secondary sets could be flanker or slot.

Winged "T" Offenses developed during the 50s that combined singlewing blocking with "T" backfield techniques.

Wishbone Formation The current set from which the triple option is run.

Zone The five areas into which the defensive secondary is divided.

Zone Coverage An area type of defensive coverage.

Index

T